"As someone who has worked with many family members over the years, I've found that this book offers practical and valuable advice."

    —PAUL ORFALEA, *Founder and Chairperson of Kinko's*

"This is a valuable book for anyone engaged in any aspect of a family firm, both for the book's insights and the thoughts inspired by the many valuable observations. This book will help all generations deal with the joys and sorrows of the family business."

    —BROOKS FIRESTONE, *Firestone Tire & Rubber Company and The Firestone Vineyard*

"Having a family-owned business can be more challenging than driving at 200 mph. This book is a roadmap that helps businesses win the race."

    —PARNELLI JONES, *President and CEO of Sports VIP's Inc., and former winner of the Indy 500*

Keep the Family Baggage Out of the Family Business

*Avoiding the
Seven Deadly Sins
That Destroy
Family Businesses*

QUENTIN J. FLEMING

A FIRESIDE BOOK
Published by Simon & Schuster

F

FIRESIDE
Rockefeller Center
1230 Avenue of the Americas
New York, NY 10020

Copyright © 2000 by Quentin J. Fleming
FIRESIDE and colophon are registered trademarks
of Simon & Schuster Inc.

Designed by Pagesetters Inc.

Manufactured in the United States of America

1   3   5   7   9   10   8   6   4   2

Library of Congress Cataloging-in-Publication Data
Fleming, Quentin J.
Keep the family baggage out of the family business : avoiding the seven
deadly sins that destroy family buisness / Quentin J. Fleming.
p. cm.
1. Family corporation—Management. 2. Family-owned business enterprises—Management. 3. Family-owned business enterprises—Law and
legislation. 4. Communication in the family. 5. Domestic relations. I: Title.
HD62.25 .F59 2000
658'.045—dc21
99-44139
CIP
ISBN 0-684-85604-2

"Do Not Go Gentle Into That Good Night" by Dylan Thomas, from *The
Poems of Dylan Thomas*. Copyright © 1952 by Dylan Thomas. Reprinted
by permission of New Directions Publishing Corp.
and David Higham Associates Limited.

Contents

PART III

Succession:

A Battleground unto Itself

PART IV

It Comes with the Territory:

Other Problems Inherent in Family Businesses

PART V

All Is Not Lost:

Recommendations and Solutions

PART I

....

What's Causing This Mess?

....

The Family System,
the Business System, and
the Accompanying Baggage

Poor George Bailey, lead character of the movie *It's a Wonderful Life*. He wanted to commit suicide. Why? I think it had something to do with being forced to work in a family business. It makes you wonder just how wonderful his life was.

When we first meet George, he's young, talented, and full of life, talking about wanting to travel the world and all the things he would build. But this is not to be. As the oldest son in the family, he's obligated to step in and run his family's business when his father dies unexpectedly.

And what about his younger brother? Harry gets to go off to college. The same with George's good friend Sam: he goes away, chases his dreams, and becomes successful, happy, and wealthy. But not George. He's forced to quash his dreams, stay in his hometown, operate his family's business (which he has no interest in), and employ family members of questionable competence.

While many think the movie is about the difference George made on the people of his town and how the world would have been different had he never been born, the *true* message of the movie is that it was a tragedy that George didn't go off and pursue his dreams. George was a wonderful person, but no one who's seen the movie stops to realize how many more people's lives George Bailey would have touched had he been free to leave the family's business—how much better the world would have been on an even larger scale. *That* would have been a wonderful life.

You don't want to be like George Bailey: forced into a family business and a career you don't want while having to employ a worthless relative like Uncle Billy down at the Building & Loan. The holidays are traumatic enough without losing $8,000.

Decades ago the word "cancer" was mentioned only in whispers. This "C-word" was not to be uttered. If a person was diagnosed with cancer, doctors would often instruct family members not to tell him or her the diagnosis. Today, people matter-of-factly say, "I've got cancer," and it's one of the reasons that the survival rate is increasing: they deal with the problem head-on and overcome it.

Today, in business, there's something that I call the "F-word," and in many circumstances it can be vulgar. The word is "family." Working in a business with your family is a dangerous proposition—both for the business and for family relationships—and it's time that people begin to talk about it. The only way to increase the survival rate for family businesses is to deal with the problem head-on.

This book is going to help you achieve your full potential

and live a wonderful life. Rather than sacrifice your dreams to a family business as George did, you'll learn that there are other options available to you and your loved ones. If you do decide to work in your family's business, you will understand the problems unique to a family business, and you will be able to address—and overcome—them.

1

.....

Why You Need to Read This Book

As a consultant, I am continually being told by people in family businesses that they are unsophisticated and that their lack of expertise on many business matters is hurting them. I disagree. The main thing that is hurting family businesses is the family.

A Quick Overview of Family Businesses

WHAT IS A FAMILY BUSINESS?

This book uses a simple definition of a family business: *Any instance in which two or more people from the same family work together in a business that at least one of them owns.* It may be a combination of husband and wife, father and son, brothers, dad and his distant cousins, and so on. This definition is used because anytime family members work together they face a unique set of problems.

HOW MANY ARE THERE?

Family businesses are the greatest stealth phenomenon in the U.S. economy. Accordingly, statistics for these businesses are fuzzy. The federal government does not track "family business" as a category in its census data. You can obtain information on the relative size and number of businesses, business ownership by ethnicity, number of home-based businesses, and so forth. But there's no straightforward count of family businesses.

Some estimates state that there are more than 12 million family businesses in the United States, while others are that family businesses:

- Make up 75 to 95 percent of all U.S. companies
- Generate 40 to 60 percent of gross national product
- Represent more than half of all wages paid
- Make up one third of *Fortune* 500 companies and almost two thirds of all companies traded on the New York Stock Exchange

Family businesses are *the* major force in our economy. Instead of focusing on quarterly earnings estimates, unemployment statistics, or the Dow Jones Industrial Average, the business media should focus on family businesses, since the health of family businesses affects and reflects the health of our economy.

MOST OF THEM DON'T SURVIVE

The probability that a family business will survive long enough to be handed to the next generation is not great. Consider these statistics:

- Approximately 30 percent will survive to the second generation.
- Only 10 percent will survive to the third generation.

AND SOME BIG CHANGES ARE IN STORE

In the next five years, approximately one third of family businesses will undergo succession—that is, control of the business will pass from one family member to another. Most of these businesses will face serious problems during succession, and many of them won't survive. Even those businesses that survive succession don't necessarily thrive and may not survive long enough to be handed over to the next generation.

It Ain't Easy Being a Family Business

There is an almost universal misperception that people in family businesses have it easy: they own their own business, automatically get jobs, and don't have to worry about losing their jobs in a downsizing.

THE MULTIPLE BURDENS FACING PARENTS IN A FAMILY BUSINESS

The owners of a family business are often the parents. As such, they have to contend with the stresses and strains of running a business *and* raising children.

An owner has to keep the business viable. The owner's economic survival is usually dependent upon the business. But since it's a family business, the family that's dependent upon the business is not necessarily restricted to the nuclear family.

Children, aunts and uncles, cousins, and stepchildren may all be dependent upon this business for a paycheck.

In addition to short-run economic survival, a family business often represents a legacy to be handed down to succeeding generations. This adds pressure to keep the business viable beyond its value as an economic asset, as a valuable part of the family's heritage.

Employer to family, extended family, and nonfamily members. The owner is an employer and thus must perform many traditional supervisory tasks. What makes this tricky is the diverse cast of characters who are employed, often ranging from immediate family members to complete strangers. How can these supervisory tasks be performed in a way that is fair to all?

Family-business owners must maintain an environment that promotes fairness to all; otherwise there is the danger of giving preferential treatment to family members. Besides decreasing the motivation of nonfamily employees, in our lawsuit-happy world it raises the specter of being hit with a labor grievance.

Being a parent. In addition to running the business, the owners are also supposed to raise their children. When do the parents find the time to be parents when they're consumed with running the business?

If their children are to grow into healthy adults and enter the family business (or go to work anywhere else, for that matter), they need to learn a series of business skills and character traits that require the active tutelage of their parents.

Being a spouse. Marriage is supposed to be a partnership, and when a family business is involved, it's not uncommon for the partners to become coworkers. How can you maintain a vibrant and healthy marriage when you're forced to spend your working hours confronting the countless pressures presented by running the family's business in addition to the normal pressures of raising your family?

HOW MANY HATS CAN ONE PERSON WEAR?

In most situations you're deemed to have a mental illness if you have multiple personalities, yet if you work in your family's business you're forced to have multiple identities and people expect you to be sane. But how sane can you be when you are forced to embody at least two of four separate and distinct identities, and each of these identities creates conflicting demands?

There are three things to remember when examining Figure 1. First, every family member who is involved with the family business is wearing at least two hats. Everyone wears the hat of a family member, plus whatever other hat or hats his or her business involvement dictates. Second, each role provides a different perspective on the business, all of which are correct. Third, the perspective for each of these identities is usually very different. This multiplicity of roles and perspectives can create confusion, conflict, and tension.

Family member. Family membership is automatic, so whether they want it or not, any family member working in the family business automatically has this identity. But the roles and responsibilities of being a family member do not have anything to do with running a business. In fact, these roles and responsibilities often get in the way of running an effective business.

FIGURE 1

Multiple Hats That May Be Worn

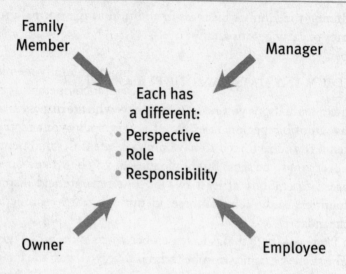

Family Member

Manager

Each has
a different:
• Perspective
• Role
• Responsibility

Owner

Employee

Owner. A person with an ownership interest looks at the business from the perspective of someone with an asset to protect and to derive profit from. But there are varying types of ownership, and each of these can create a differing set of problems.

A person's ownership interest might involve active control, or it might be a limited or passive investment with no control over the company's operations. Owners lacking formal control may create conflict when they try to influence the business by exerting pressure on the family members who do have control of the business.

In addition, if an owner does not work for the family business, his or her perceived economic benefits from ownership might be very much at odds with those of people who draw salaries from the business. One person will be arguing for dividends while the other says that profits need to be reinvested.

Manager. Although in the abstract, appointment to management should be based on merit, many families put family members in management without regard to aptitude, creating tension between competent and incompetent family members (as well as competent employees and incompetent family members). In addition, family members who are managers may have conflicting business priorities that spill over and create tense family interactions.

Family members who manage the business may be in conflict with those owning it, especially when those responsible for running the business do not have sufficient power to take the actions they want.

Employee. So what happens to family members who have been relegated to employee status? How do they react, knowing their family's name is on the door yet they've been relegated to worker bee?

Lacking ownership or management power, these employees often resort to "The Whine Factor" to overcome a lack of formal authority. They will exploit their membership in the family, whining as loudly as possible to try to exert informal control over business activities. Their failure to contain themselves within a limited business role creates conflict.

WHY WORK IN A FAMILY BUSINESS?

To carry on the family tradition. The family takes great pride in its business, and it's an important element in defining who it is. As such, family members feel it's their duty to enter the business and keep it running.

It's a matter of destiny. Each family has its own set of beliefs, and when a family owns a business, this often includes a belief that family members are supposed to work for it. The children are often taught that their destiny is to eventually succeed their parents in the business.

There's a lot more freedom than in working for a big company. Many people think that working for a big company is repressive—and they're right! They believe that working in their family's business will provide them with greater responsibility and authority, the opportunity to learn and handle diverse roles, and the ability to have a much larger impact than if they were just another employee at a big company.

The business helps unite the family. Some families truly enjoy being a family. What better way for the family to face the challenges of the world than to rally their strengths behind the family business? These families believe that running the business provides a forum to promote family closeness.

ADVANTAGES OF EMPLOYING FAMILY MEMBERS

Family members are more likely to "fit in." Every business has its own culture. In a family business, this culture usually reflects the family itself. Employing a family member means employing someone who already fits in. This person will likely share similar values, beliefs, and attitudes with both the family and the employer (since they're the same). Because family businesses are often quite small, compatibility is important.

They're more committed to the business and its success. Family members are often aware of just how much their family depends upon the business for its livelihood. They also understand just how devastating the business's failure could be to their family. This desire to protect the family's economic livelihood—if not the family itself—helps commit them to the business's success.

An emphasis on relationships. Family members usually feel a strong bond with their family's values and traditions and will work to maintain these within the business.

Values and traditions found in family businesses often include a strong desire to develop and maintain close relationships, and when this involves customers, it usually helps to create goodwill. Research has shown that many customers actually prefer dealing with a family business because of this goodwill. Family members are also more likely to be protective of the family's name and reputation, helping to maintain the business's goodwill.

POTENTIAL DRAWBACKS OF EMPLOYING FAMILY MEMBERS

Competency is not included in the manufacturer's warranty. Hiring someone based solely on his or her status as a family member fails to address the issue of whether this person is competent or not. If the business must hire someone from within the family, it might be choosing the lesser of two evils rather than finding the best possible candidate.

Even if some family members are competent, there's no guarantee that the hiring individual will be able to determine who they are because it is often difficult to obtain honest or accurate feedback regarding the candidates' potential. Non-family employees within the business may be fearful of giving honest feedback because they may be criticizing someone who is both a family member and a potential future boss.

"The Family Ceiling." Women in the corporate world have long known that there's a "glass ceiling"—an invisible barrier that prevents their rising above a certain level within companies. Ironically, there's an identical barrier facing nonfamily employees who work in family businesses. I call it the "family ceiling." It's a very real barrier that few nonfamily employees will ever pass.

Family businesses usually reserve the top positions for family members. I'm not saying that this is wrong. After all, the business is owned by the family and it's their prerogative. But reserving the top positions for family members does not guarantee that the most competent people in the organization will be at the top. In addition, nonfamily employees who are talented will be forced to go elsewhere if they want to attain a top title.

If you think it's hard to fire a civil servant, try firing a family member. A family member working in a family business possesses a unique weapon against getting fired: family membership.

Firing a family member involves more than firing the person. It can create a family incident that disrupts the entire family as the person being fired turns to other family members for protection. Just imagine the dinner table during the next holidays, when the fired family member sits next to former coworkers.

2

......

Systems and Baggage

Why are family businesses having trouble? The answer to this critical question boils down to two words: systems and baggage.

Systems refer to all things that go into how a family or a business operates: the ways in which people interact with one another and their interrelationships and interdependencies. Every family is a system unto itself, and so is every business. But in a family business, the interaction of the family and the business systems can be a potential knockout punch to the business.

Baggage, in this case, is not something you buy in a department store. Baggage can be the death blow to a family business. **Understanding what systems and baggage are and how they affect your family's business can help you understand—and solve—your family business's problems.**

The Family Business System(s)

There are always two completely different and distinct systems involved in a family business. The first is the *family system;* and the second is the *business system*. That's the problem.

When a family works together, it inevitably blends the two systems by imposing the family system onto the business. A family business is supposed to be a business, and as such it is supposed to be controlled by its business system. It isn't. The family begins to "play family" in the business by re-creating its family system there. To say that this creates problems is an understatement.

For a family to be healthy, it needs to have a family system that operates in a particular way. For a business to be healthy (or successful) it needs its business system to operate in a particular way. **The attributes of a healthy business system are usually at complete odds with the attributes of a healthy family system.**

FOR EVERY ACTION, THERE WILL BE AN EQUAL AND OPPOSITE REACTION

In a perfect world, the family system and the business system would function separately and independently from each other, with their own dynamics, rules, expectations, members, and so on. Unfortunately, with a family business, this doesn't happen, and this is illustrated in Figure 2.

What happens in each of these systems independently will inevitably impact the other system, which in turn reacts and impacts the other system, and so on. In other words, whatever happens in the family system impacts the business system, and whatever happens in the business system spills over into the family system. The cycle repeats indefinitely.

FAMILY SYSTEMS VERSUS BUSINESS SYSTEMS

Forget about men and women being from different planets; family and business systems are from opposing universes.

FIGURE 2

The Family Business System(s)

**Relationships, roles, issues,
emotions, history, etc.,
impact the business's activities.**

Family   **Business**

**Participation in and/or ownership
of the business
impacts family relations.**

A quick examination of the accompanying table demonstrates that the attributes of a healthy family system are diametrically opposed to the attributes of an effective business system.

Business systems exist to further the business. Thus these systems require clear definitions and strict adherence. The family system exists to help individual family members. While a complete lack of clarity creates a dysfunctional family, healthy family systems generally leave many dimensions vague, requiring give-and-take and compromise.

There's a reason family members aren't allowed to serve in the same military unit. U.S. military policy prohibits family members from serving in the same combat unit. In World War II the navy allowed brothers to serve on the same ships, thinking it

Family Systems Versus Business Systems

Dimension	Healthy Family System	Effective Business System
Membership (and tenure)	Inclusion in system is automatic based upon birth, marriage, adoption, etc. Membership almost always lasts indefinitely (i.e., unless members do something to alienate themselves.)	People are included in the system only after it has been determined that there is a legitimate business need for the role and the person has been selected for inclusion. Membership exists only so long as there is a business need for the role and is always contingent upon satisfactory performance.
"Who's in charge?"	Leadership shifts among family members, depending upon the situation. There is no overwhelming need for any person to feel that they must be in charge.	There is a single entity with final authority (e.g., owner, CEO, board of directors), and all members are ultimately responsible to this person or body.
Decision making	Decision-making authority shifts according to the situation. Parents maintain a unified position vis-à-vis the children.	Decision-making authority is clearly defined and consistent.

Family Systems Versus Business Systems (*continued*)

Dimension	Healthy Family System	Effective Business System
Reporting relationships (i.e., who they take orders from and are accountable to)	Expectations regarding authority and accountability continually shift according to the specific situation. It is possible for the orientation to reverse in certain situations (e.g., parents may become accountable to children).	Each person has a clearly defined reporting relationship to a boss (best if a single boss) and others in the organization. Relationships must be strictly adhered to.
Job definition (i.e., roles)	People have "titles" according to marriage or birth, but the tasks they are expected to perform are determined in accordance with each person's capabilities. Relationships vis-à-vis others shifts according to the situation and over time.	There is a clearly defined reason for the position to exist (i.e., it exists to support the organization) and a set of tasks to be performed, based on fulfilling the organization's needs. The relationship of each job to other jobs in the business is clearly delineated.
Priorities	Each individual's long-range goal takes precedence, to the extent that it does not undermine the legitimate needs or interests of other family members.	There is a uniform, long-range goal for the organization. All units (e.g., divisions, departments, people) make their plans solely to further this goal, subjugating their own needs if necessary.

Family Systems Versus Business Systems (*continued*)

Dimension	Healthy Family System	Effective Business System
Goals and performance evaluation criteria	Goals are informal, evolving around personal hopes and aspirations. They may be explicit and clearly defined, but there is no rigid, formal performance evaluation process. Goals focus on individual and collective growth, rather than subserviently serving the family unit.	Formal goals are clearly defined and established at the beginning of each planning cycle with the purpose of supporting the organization. People are held accountable for meeting their goals, and there is a formal evaluation of performance and feedback is given. Rewards and/or punishment are directly related to this evaluation.
Rewards	Emphasize love and nurturing from other family members, and provide greater freedom for self-actualization.	Emphasize compensation or greater authority/ autonomy.
Longevity	The family will always exist as a family, but the goal is to separate and have the children start their own nuclear families.	The organization will exist only as long as the business exists, but the goal is to keep the unit together and going indefinitely.

was good for morale, until families began to lose several sons when a ship was destroyed. In one instance, a single family lost all of its five sons.

What's the connection to a family business? Every business can be thought of as an army engaged in a life-and-death battle in its own marketplace. There are offensive and defensive moves, attacks, counterattacks, preemptive strikes—and casualties. You don't want an entire family wiped out because its business is defeated in the marketplace battlefield.

If you take another look at the table, you'll see that an effective business system puts the interests of the business ahead of the best interests of its people, even if it means having to "take casualties." But healthy family systems avoid casualties.

Family businesses get into trouble because the family system does not always allow the business system to do what's required for the business to succeed or, sometimes, survive.

Whose needs take priority—the business's or the people's? In a traditional business system, the business comes first and personal needs are secondary. In a business controlled by the family system, the business is viewed as a vehicle to serve the family's needs. As a result, families owning businesses tend to feel that their personal needs take precedence over any needs of the business. They will use their business as a tool to fund their pet projects.

What criteria will be used to make decisions? In a traditional business system, the prevailing value is "It's best for the company." Decisions are based upon rational facts, and personal or emotional considerations are to be kept out.

In a family system, the criterion applied to decisions is "What's best for our family?" As a result, emotion-based concerns are interjected into the decision-making process and take priority over rational thinking (and best business practices).

Baggage

WHAT IS FAMILY BAGGAGE?

"Baggage" is a term used by psychologists to describe problems that people carry with them. It's an effective metaphor because these problems hamper people's ability to interact, cope, or behave appropriately. They react to their baggage, not to the actual situation. For example, a child who was molested may not be able to achieve intimacy in his or her relationships as an adult; a person who was spoiled has unrealistic expectations.

What does baggage have to do with family businesses? Think for a moment about the countless tensions, quarrels, jealousies, and small rivalries that naturally arise in the course of daily life, even in healthy families. When a family works together, it all comes into the business. **The impact of family baggage in a family business is the unacknowledged root cause of almost every problem affecting it.** Despite the largely unspoken nature of this problem, it must be addressed if family businesses are to survive and achieve the success they deserve.

To help illustrate this point, I've identified certain "universal truths" that apply to any family's baggage.

Universal Truths About Your Family's Baggage

- It's always heavier than it looks.
- It doesn't come with rollers; you're forced to carry it.
- You can't pay a skycap enough to want to carry it.

- You can't lose it forever by checking it in with the airlines.
- The baggage usually flies first class, while you're stuck in coach.
- There is no inherent value in having a matched set (regardless of the snob appeal).
- It comes with your initials engraved on it.
- It likes to pop open and dump your underwear out for everyone to see.
- No matter how carefully you pack, your most precious items will get crushed.
- The American Tourister gorilla is afraid to go near it.
- After seventy-five years they weren't able to retrieve any bodies from the *Titanic,* but a lot of the baggage was recovered in pretty good shape.

THE PEOPLE WHO MAKE THE MOST SENSE

A close friend who is a psychiatrist once let me in on a secret that is helpful for understanding human behavior and that has served me well as a consultant: *The people whose behavior makes the most sense are those who are "truly crazy"—once you crack the code.*

Contrary to what most people think, the people whose behavior makes the most sense are not the people holding the most responsible positions in the community, who put on business suits and go to work. Rather, it's the people who have been institutionalized. The secret is that you have to understand their reality (i.e., the code). Once a psychiatrist cracks this code, everything these people do makes perfect sense.

It's the people walking around in their business suits who, conversely, often make no sense. Their built-in defenses to problems produce convoluted behaviors. Truly crazy people don't have these defenses—their actions are pure responses to what they believe is happening.

FAMILY BAGGAGE IS "THE CODE" IN FAMILY BUSINESSES

Whenever I am advising a family business, the challenge is to understand what is really happening in that organization. The secret of success is discovering the root cause of their problems, and this occurs once I've "cracked the code." "The Golden Rule of Family Baggage" (see box) represents the code in any family business. Using this rule, all behavior within any family business makes sense. The key to success for any family business is to identify, then eliminate the family baggage from the family business.

The Golden Rule of Family Baggage

Without deliberate intervention, any conflicts, tensions, disagreements, or dysfunctional patterns that exist in the family environment will be brought into the business environment.

The "Seven Deadly Sins" that are presented later in this book are derived directly from the Golden Rule of Family Baggage and represent the most common manifestations of the family baggage. Family businesses suffering from these syndromes are acting in a manner that makes sense within the context of what is driving the family system.

WHAT ARE BUSINESS ADVISORS OVERLOOKING?

Most business advisors fail to crack the code when working with family businesses, limiting their attention to the business system and ignoring what is occurring within the family system. Either they do not understand that these issues exist, or they do not feel comfortable addressing them. The result is that the root cause of most problems within the business system is never properly addressed.

Limiting intervention to making changes in the business system is seldom effective because the source of the problem—the baggage in the family system—has not been addressed. Thus the changes made to the business system actually accommodate the family's baggage rather than impose best business practices.

Forget About Church and State: Separate the Family and the Business

What can family businesses do to protect themselves from the destructive interplay of family and business systems as well as family baggage?

Principle 1: The Chances of a Family Business Being Successful Are Significantly Improved When Sentimental and Emotional Considerations <u>Are Removed from</u> Decisions Made and Actions Taken

This principle forces the family to acknowledge that it is operating a business and that decisions should be based upon sound business criteria.

The family system will continually try to impose sentimental and emotional considerations on the decision-making process. Don't let it.

Principle 2: The Chances of a Family Business Being Successful Are Significantly Improved by <u>Recognizing the Impact of</u> Sentimental and Emotional Factors

The sentimental and emotional factors that emerge from the family system will act to derail the family's business. These factors are so pervasive that most people in family businesses are unaware of them. Worse, if they do know they're there, they may assume they're normal and are supposed to be used in business.

This second principle suggests making family members aware that these factors are creeping into the business. It is important that they be uncovered, addressed, and resolved. Sometimes it's only by recognizing their existence that the family is able to apply the first principle and remove them from decisions and actions.

3

When Worlds Collide: The Family System Meets the Business System

What are the most common business problems created by the family system? Why do conflicts in family businesses possess an intensity that is seldom seen in non-family-owned businesses? Understanding the answers to these questions provides family members and business advisors with critical insight to help promote success.

When the Family's System Drives Its Business's Behavior

Running a business is fundamentally different from raising a family, and it creates serious problems for the business when the family tries to run the business the same way it does the family. Yet this is what many family businesses do: they unknowingly apply family practices to the conduct of their business.

You've seen how the practices of a healthy family system

differ from those of an effective business system. The accompanying box illustrates how this commingling of systems hampers the business.

The Impact of Using the Family System Model in the Business System

Dimension	Family System Definition	Effect on the Business System
Membership (and tenure)	People are automatically included in the system and remain in it indefinitely.	Family members are automatically brought into the business regardless of whether there's a need for them or whether they're qualified for the position. They enjoy lifetime tenure regardless of their job performance or adverse impact on the business.
"Who's in charge?"	Authority is a collaborative process.	All people feel entitled to have a say in the business's affairs, regardless of their legitimacy or qualifications.
Decision making	A decision may be made by several persons, depending upon the situation. The system for determining the decision maker is informal.	There is no clear-cut person entitled to make decisions on particular matters. Everyone seems to think that they should be allowed to decide.

The Impact of Using the Family System Model in the Business System (*continued*)

Dimension	Family System Definition	Effect on the Business System
Reporting relationships (i.e., who people take orders from and are accountable to)	There is a flexible hierarchy, continually shifting according to the situation.	There is a lack of a clear-cut hierarchy, and people cannot be held accountable.
Job definition (i.e., roles)	People do tasks (i.e., chores) in accordance with what they want to do. Some tasks get done, others don't.	People feel entitled to perform the types of assignments they want, rather than based upon what the business needs.
Priorities	The needs of the people within the system take priority over the system.	People expect that the business will support their individual long-range goals and accommodate their personal needs.
Goals and performance evaluation criteria	People make general, informal long-range goals focused on meeting their individual needs, and these are primarily a personal matter.	People do not receive performance-related goals designed to support the business's needs. There's nothing to be held accountable for.

The Impact of Using the Family System
Model in the Business System (*continued*)

Dimension	Family System Definition	Effect on the Business System
Rewards	Rewards are given to make people feel loved by the family.	People are automatically rewarded to make them feel loved regardless of their job performance.
Longevity	The system (i.e., family) has always existed and will continue to do so.	People assume that the business will automatically perpetuate itself and see no reason for changes or improvements (i.e., to act like a business).

Although imposing the family system onto the business's operation creates a series of problems, the solution is straightforward: the business must be run like a business, and this means applying effective business practices. This is not easy, even if the owner understands what needs to be done. Some family members will refuse to understand, and they will do everything possible to impose the family system onto the business.

The Conflict When Systems Overlap

SOURCES OF CONFLICT FOR PEOPLE WHO ARE NOT IN A FAMILY BUSINESS

People in nonfamily businesses find that conflicts emanate from two different sources. Each source presents its own type of conflict in its own venue, and fortunately, each can be handled separately. These differing sources and types of conflict are shown in Figure 3.

When a person is not involved in a family business, family squabbles stay at home in the family and professional disagreements stay at work, except to the extent that Dad might go to work and dump on his employees or come home and kick the dog.

FIGURE 3

Sources of Conflict for People Who Are
Not in a Family Business

Family System   Business System

Family   Professional
squabbles   disagreements

Usually emotion-based   Usually logic-based
Stay at home   Stay at work

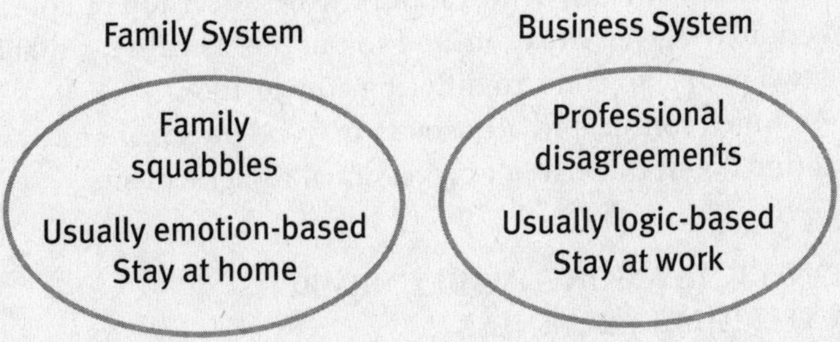

FAMILY SQUABBLES

All family members fight from time to time. It's inevitable and, within limits, actually healthy, so long as it's merely a squabble and not a deep, pathological conflict. Family squabbles originate in the family system and are emotionally based. They are often the result of too little *distance*.

Resolving these squabbles usually doesn't require making changes. It's a matter of people letting off a little steam and then calming down. Since the conflict has an emotional basis, cold reason does nothing to end it. They just need to give each other some space and let the situation cool down.

PROFESSIONAL DISAGREEMENTS

Professional disagreements are conflicts that occur within the business system. Two (or more) people will consider a given situation and have conflicting opinions.

The critical distinction is that the focus of the conflict is limited to the business system. It emanates from the interpretation of a given set of facts, beliefs about the best decision or course of action in a given situation, and so on. It is usually legitimate for two people to come to differing conclusions.

At times conflicts in a business may be personal and thus emotional, but these aren't professional disagreements.

CONFLICTS AMONG FAMILY MEMBERS
IN THE FAMILY BUSINESS

Figure 4 illustrates what happens in family businesses. The elements are the same as those in Figure 3, but an entirely new dimension is created that is unique to family businesses. Because the coworkers are also family members, their dis-

---

FIGURE 4

The Conflict When Systems Overlap

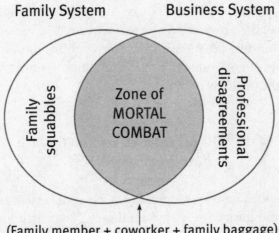

Family System   Business System

Family squabbles

Zone of MORTAL COMBAT

Professional disagreements

(Family member + coworker + family baggage)

agreements are never either/or situations. Instead, conflict is produced by overlapping family and business systems.

The resulting conflict enters the "Zone of Mortal Combat." It's no longer a matter of who's right or wrong; it's about not losing and punishing one's mortal enemies (i.e., opponents). The more the circles in Figure 4 overlap, the more mortal the combat becomes. In some families, the two circles overlap so much they become one.

Fights in the Zone of Mortal Combat are based on emotion, and the intensity of emotion feeds the destructiveness of the fighting. No amount of logic or reason can prevail. Although these fights are based on emotion (and how can they not be when both the family system and the family baggage are involved?), people deceive themselves into believing that they are engaged in a work-related fight. They will keep grabbing at data, reports, spreadsheets, statistics, and so on, to prove they're right. But no amount of logic will prevail in an emotionally based situation, and the fact that their logic fails to persuade their combatant only enrages them more.

Once people enter the Zone of Mortal Combat, fights take on a life of their own and may continue until both sides die (literally). In some situations people keep fighting until the company goes out of business and then continue fighting over who caused the business to fail.

Are You a FAMILY Business or a Family BUSINESS?

The accompanying questionnaire assesses the extent to which family and business systems are driving your own business's actions. It is an important indicator of your business's health, analogous to going to the doctor for a checkup.

Photocopy the questionnaire, and administer it to yourself. Then administer it to several family members within your business. Do your scores agree? Finally, as a reality check, and only if *they* feel comfortable, have several nonfamily members complete the questionnaire. Their input can be invaluable (so long as it's safe for them to be honest).

Once you have completed the survey, determine your score. If your score is 30 or more, you're operating a healthy business. 20 to 29 means that your family system is exerting too much control over how you are operating your business. If your score is less than 20, your business is in very serious trouble or soon will be. You must take immediate steps to strengthen your business, and you will learn how as you read this book.

Are You a FAMILY Business or a Family BUSINESS?

Y or N

1. It is imperative that the business be kept intact and handed over to the children. _____

2. Family members are careful to avoid discussing family matters at work. _____

3. Family members are paid equally. _____

4. Children live apart from the family for an extended number of years prior to their entry into the family's business. _____

5. The business will hire a better-qualified outsider before it will employ a family member. _____

6. The business is a tool that helps keep the family together. _____

7. Jobs and roles are assigned to family members working in the business without regard to gender. _____

8. The activities and happenings of the business are a constant subject of attention and/or conversation throughout the family. _____

9. Many of the ideas and solutions that are used to improve the business and/or solve problems come from the children. _____

10. Everyone is evaluated and rewarded strictly on their job performance. _____

11. Family members engage in behaviors that would not be tolerated in any other company. _____

12. The children working in the business are able to (and do) make decisions without hesitation. _____

Y or N

13. The best interest of the business always takes precedence over family members' desires. _____

14. It's important for the business that family members get along and allow problems to resolve themselves over time. _____

15. In-laws and spouses (i.e., nonblood family members) are involved in business matters. _____

16. "Only family members have the commitment we need to make our business a success." _____

17. People in the business have clearly defined roles, accompanied with full and proper authority. _____

18. Prospective successors are deliberately involved in development activities outside of the company to help strengthen their skills. _____

19. There are multiple generations of family members actively involved in the business and the oldest generation is firmly calling the shots. _____

20. The business owner ignores the possible impact upon family members when making decisions. _____

21. It's assumed that the children will come work for the business. _____

22. Loyalty to the family is considered a critical trait among senior managers. _____

Y or N

23. Children having a history of deep-seated conflict will be/have been brought into the business and/or given ownership. _____

24. Business advisors tend to be old friends of the family. _____

25. Family members only receive jobs for which they are qualified. _____

26. Everyone working in the business is held strictly accountable for their job performance. _____

27. Birth order is not a factor in determining job assignments and roles. _____

28. The senior managers have been employed for many, many years by the company, and the team has been in place for a long time. _____

29. The children are (were) encouraged to pursue careers outside of the business. _____

30. Family members are used as administrators/trustees of the family's estate. _____

31. Clear boundaries are not drawn around people marrying into the family regarding their involvement/participation in the family's business. _____

32. Family members are careful to avoid relating to each other as family members while at work. _____

33. The children working in the family's business spent several years working for other companies. _____

34. Everyone working in the business is paid prevailing market wages and perks for the work they perform. _____

Y or N

35. The owners are prepared to sell the business
    if they don't believe family members can
    effectively run it in their absence. _____

Scoring the Questionnaire

Step 1
Give yourself one point for each time you
answered as follows: _____

Line 1

Yes to questions 2, 4, 5, 7, 9, 10, 12, 13, 17,
18, 20, 25, 26, 27, 29, 32, 33, 34, 35

No to questions 1, 3, 6, 8, 11, 14, 15, 16, 19,
21, 22, 23, 24, 28, 31

Step 2
Give yourself one point for each time you
answered as follows: _____

Line 2

Yes to questions 1, 3, 6, 8, 11, 14, 15, 16,
19, 21, 22, 23, 24, 28, 30, 31

No to questions 2, 4, 5, 7, 9, 10, 12, 13, 17,
18, 20, 25, 26, 27, 29, 32, 33, 34, 35

Step 3
Subtract Line 2 from Line 1 _____

PART II

We Have Seen the Enemy, and He Is Us

The Seven Deadly Sins That Destroy Family Businesses

Seven deadly sins are presented in the Bible. Family businesses have their own set of deadly sins, and there are seven of them as well. These sins occur when the family's baggage is allowed to run rampant through its business. When a family commits one of these sins, it creates problems that can result in destruction on the scale of a Cecil B. DeMille epic.

These deadly sins are the heart of this book. I've found at least one of them present in every instance of a family business failure. They are deadly—very deadly—and your business is not immune.

The Seven Deadly Sins That Destroy Family Businesses

Syndrome	Consequence
"It's the same old song"	People's behaviors, roles, and beliefs from childhood are perpetuated in the business.
"We're one big, happy family"	Failure to acknowledge that the business system requires different practices than the family system.
"They may have become adults, but they'll always be my children"	Parents are unable to accept their children as grown adults.
"You're not loyal to this family if you insist on being selfish"	Failure to acknowledge family members as individuals.
"Father knows best?"	Business founders usually possess dominating personalities and/or are consumed with the business.
"Maybe it will go away if we ignore it"	Failing to address problems that will inevitably emerge with increasing intensity and destructive potential.
"Tell me about your childhood"	Children enter the family's business before experiencing sufficient distance to resolve critical issues from their childhood.

4

....

"It's the Same Old Song"

Things that happen in a family seem to recur in its business. While that's true of all of the syndromes, it's especially true here, where we're focusing on behavior patterns that are developed in childhood.

"If You Don't . . . I'm Gonna Hold My Breath"

His parents claimed he had a stronger set of lungs than any other baby. The whole house shook when he cried. And somehow Johnny never seemed to get past the "terrible twos."

His parents ascribed it to a strong will: "He'd get an idea in his head, and that's what he wanted. No amount of coaxing could get him to change his mind." (Too bad they didn't believe in spanking.)

And talk about a temper! If he didn't get what he wanted, he'd start screaming and throwing things. "I hate you! I hate you! No fair!" The only way they could get him to stop was to give in.

Today, Johnny is thirty-five years old and the VP in charge of the family's East Valley branch office. It was always a successful operation, but somehow things have been changing since he took over. Business is slipping and a lot of the employees have departed, but it's probably due to the auto assembly plant's closing and the subsequent layoffs in that community. Johnny says he needs additional funds so he can turn the situation around and is angry that his father is asking him so many questions.

HOW DO I GET ATTENTION IN THIS FAMILY?

Let's blame it on the parents. They were too busy to give this child proper attention, so the kid had to resort to acting up to be noticed. Or maybe they were too invested in themselves to be bothered to take the time to instill proper discipline, so giving in to the kid was the easy way. Or maybe they just didn't have the resolve to assert themselves and establish control over this child. Whatever the reason, they perpetually rewarded their kid's bad behavior by giving him whatever he wanted. Forget about kids and drugs, Nancy Reagan should have taught these parents to "Just say no."

Such kids will not grow up and become well-behaved adults. As long as they're interacting with family members, they are likely to continue this pattern.

ACTING UP, ADULT STYLE

Nothing will change when these children (now adults) enter their families' businesses. They will continue to act up in order to get their way. And as adults, they learn to engage in this conduct on a more grown-up level. Screaming and yelling at the top of their lungs worked when they were two years old, but it's probably counterproductive today. Instead, they'll act up by creating problems in the workplace. The danger with this is that it's too easy to mask these problems as being legitimate responses to business situations rather than something they themselves engineer.

False crises. These overgrown children create a crisis within the business in order to get attention. When done properly, it appears as though the crisis has been generated by outside events. Once the crisis has erupted, they are in a position to issue demands to get what they want: "I need ———— to solve this crisis and save the business."

Parents never realize that the whole situation has been manufactured and that they have two possible responses to the crisis: (a) give in to their kid's demands so the crisis will disappear; or (b) fire their kid and bring someone competent in (which will prevent further crises).

A kid in a candy store. By putting this kid into the family business, parents give him a whole new arsenal of weapons with which they can be blackmailed. My advice to parents is simple: Who cares if your kid threatens to hold his breath? Let him. The worst that will happen is that he'll pass out, and no damage will be done. But this same child, now an adult and working in the family business, can destroy the business with such conduct. It cannot be tolerated under any circumstances.

The employees resent it. No one wants to work for this type of person. This person is a brat. Employees often see what the parents refuse to see, but heaven forbid they should say anything bad about this kid to the parents.

Employees with talent will depart to work elsewhere, leaving the business with the bad performers. Morale will suffer as people are forced to endure crisis after fabricated crisis.

THE EFFECT(S) OF THIS BEHAVIOR PATTERN

The business is affected by being forced to endure a series of unnecessary crises. These fabricated crises divert the business's attention away from *real* problems. In addition, employee morale suffers as people resent the brat.

"I Gave Them Everything They Ever Wanted"

All the kids loved to play at Johnny's house. He had all the latest toys. It was amazing. All he had to do was say that he wanted something, and his parents would run out and buy it. It didn't matter if things broke; they would always be replaced.

But beneath it all, something seemed wrong. All the kids said that his parents must love him because of all the neat stuff they bought him. "But why are they never here?" Johnny wondered. "They're always off at work, and I hate it."

There were other problems. It seemed that whatever he got, it wasn't quite enough. It would make him happy for a day or two; then he'd be bored with it.

As a teenager, he'd get upset when other people asked him to do things he didn't want to do. His teachers would give him homework. "But it's my time when I'm at home." At least he got to drive his new car to school.

IS THIS REALLY WHAT THEY WANTED?

Creating or running a family business is a very time-consuming endeavor. Parents often spend long hours working at the family business and have no time for their children. They often feel guilty, and to ease their feelings of guilt, they'll try to substitute money and gifts for time, attention, and love.

What they get in return is not pretty.

The children resent the parents. Even though the children may have gotten all the toys they desired, their parents failed to give emotional attention to or spend enough time with them. While the children may not express hostility directly, they often retaliate by creating problems for the parents, thereby disrupting the parents' ability to focus attention on the business.

The children resent the business. The children believe the business was the reason their parents didn't give them the attention they wanted and often wish that the business would fail. Some even try to sabotage the business.

The children become spoiled. The ugly truth is that these children are spoiled. They have no sense of personal responsibility, lack the discipline and motivation needed to be effective in business, and have a distorted sense of the value of money.

YOU'RE BRINGING THEM INTO THE BUSINESS?

Children like this are not qualified to enter their family's business for several reasons. They are what they are, and the parents are going to continue to spoil them.

They expect instant gratification. The parents taught their kids to believe that the world works as follows: They want ———; they get it immediately. Unfortunately, things don't happen this way in business; they require hard work and take time.

These expectations of immediate gratification make the children ill suited to work in the family business. In fact, they make them ill suited to work in any business, but it's worse in the family business because the parents are still there and the kid expects immediate gratification whenever the parents are in the picture.

They lack self-discipline and willpower. To accomplish anything in business, people have to start by identifying a specific goal, then set a series of detailed action steps, then apply themselves and perform these action steps.

Things don't always go according to plan. Unforeseen obstacles and setbacks will be encountered. These kids, however, expect it all to be easy and get upset at the slightest inconvenience. They simply don't have the temperament to cope with setbacks.

They have no sense of personal responsibility. These kids believe they should be able to do whatever they want with their things. And why shouldn't they? Everything has always been given to them, and if they made a mistake or misused or broke something—no problem, they'd simply get a replacement.

This pattern will continue as their parents fail to hold them accountable for what they do. Performance goals might be set, but just as there was no consequence if they broke their toys, there's no consequence for not meeting the goals.

They have a distorted sense of the value of money. Everything always came free. Isn't that how it works? The reality is that there are limits.

The family business has a finite amount of resources and money. It's usually a continual struggle between what's wanted, what's really needed, and the resources available. These kids assume that there's plenty of money for everything and often refuse to believe otherwise. And because they believe in instant gratification, they won't hesitate to use the company's resources to fulfill their own desires rather than meet the company's needs.

THE EFFECT(S) OF THIS BEHAVIOR PATTERN

When such children are employed, the family's business is carrying deadwood. The company is wasting its resources because the parents usually overpay these children with lavish salaries and perks. In addition, these children are not held accountable for their lack of performance, and others will have to be employed to clean up their messes.

"Go Play with Your Dolls"

She wasn't ever expected to be anything, except maybe beautiful to men. She couldn't explain it, but things seemed to be different for her brother. Sure, he was two years older, but he seemed to have a different role within the family.

She remembers that at family gatherings her uncles would ask her brother what he wanted to be when he grew up. "That's great," they'd say. "You've got to study hard in school so you can be sure to get to the top."

Of course, she wasn't ignored. They'd ask her about her activities, but they always seemed focused on what she had just done. "That's a really pretty dress," they'd say. Somehow, her success seemed to be related to her ability to attract a man rather than to what she could accomplish herself.

Her brother was pushed into organized sports. "You've got to get out there and be tough. Don't whine; hit them back even harder." She'd have sleep-over parties with her girlfriends. They'd laugh and giggle, play records, and read magazines.

In high school, her brother got Bs, lettered in wrestling, and was very social. The parents couldn't wait for him to go to college and enter their family business. They had big plans for him. She quietly got As, but . . .

DOUBLE STANDARDS IN A SINGLE FAMILY SYSTEM

Traditionally, boys have been raised to be boys and girls to be girls. The adults in family businesses carry notions learned during their childhood into adulthood and into the business.

Recent years have seen significant changes in women's roles in the workplace. But the generation that is benefiting from these changes is just beginning to enter their families' businesses, so although it might seem antiquated, this discussion is a closer reflection of the current situation than some might think.

Be aggressive. Push back. Win. Boys are taught not to cry; it's sissy. Instead, they are expected to be little bundles of misbehavior and aggression. They're pushed into organized sports, where they're rewarded for their physical prowess.

Boys are taught that they're supposed to be the providers, that they should go out into the world and take charge. It wasn't so long ago that textbooks told them, "In America, any boy can grow up to be president, and any girl can grow up to be Miss America."

When parents talk about the family business, they plant seeds in boys' minds that someday they will enter it and take it over.

That's sweet. Girls are expected to be cute and quiet. Just look at the way they're dressed; dresses and patent leather shoes were not designed for playing kickball on the school playground.

Girls are not encouraged to think about careers. Any expression of wanting a career in the family business is met by silence or discouragement. Instead, they're expected to be moms, to marry someone and raise the children. And if their family is really dysfunctional, they're taught that in order to be "complete" they need to have a man to take care of them.

Finally, let's not get into too much detail about the double standards about dating. Sons are expected to sow their wild oats; that's just the way boys are. But God help daughters should they engage in similar activities.

WHO'S WHO IN THE FAMILY BUSINESS

Sons and daughters continue to play the role of sons and daughters when they enter the family business.

Roles for the boys. It's automatically assumed that the boys will take over the family business (or is it their father's business?). They are put into jobs that have significant authority or that will have authority added as they mature. The employees will automatically assume that the boys are headed for the top even if it hasn't been announced.

Though their destiny is predetermined, there is a failure to address a basic question: Do the boys have the talent to do the jobs?

Roles for the girls? If they do enter the family business, the daughters are almost never considered for the top position. This is especially true if their brother is in the business, even more so if the brother is older. Baby sister just does not run the family's business. In fact, if she's married, the family might even bring her husband rather than her into the business; or, if she's already there, bring him in above her.

While their brothers are being groomed for the top, daughters will often take more junior positions within the company, ones more analogous to those of ordinary employees. While their brothers keep moving up, they may be left in their jobs and ignored.

Why should they expect to be treated differently? The family has never taken the notion of professional women seriously. To make matters worse, their brothers will find it easy to ignore them and any ideas they may offer (assuming they speak up and offer any). After all, this is what they were taught to do in their family's system.

THE EFFECT(S) OF THIS BEHAVIOR PATTERN

This behavior pattern automatically prevents the business from capitalizing on the talents of the family's daughters. Whatever capabilities they may possess and contributions they could make to the business are denied. Conversely, the business creates roles for her brothers, who might not be qualified for said roles. Such double standards also help to promote conflict among the brothers and sisters.

The "It's the Same Old Song" Syndrome

People's behaviors, roles, and beliefs from childhood are perpetuated in the business.

Manifestation	Description	Effect(s)
"If you don't . . . I'm gonna hold my breath"	Children who acted up in order to get their way.	Continue to create problems within the business in order to get their way.
"I gave them everything they ever wanted"	Parents who spoiled or indulged their children.	Continue to do so through "velvet handcuffs" or lack of accountability.
"Go play with your dolls"	Expectation of daughters to assume "traditional" domestic roles while pushing sons to be competitive.	The business is arbitrarily denied full use of all talent within the family. If participating, daughters are in subservient roles within the business.

5

......

"We're One Big, Happy Family"

Family members are family members twenty-four hours a day, seven days a week. But what happens when they insist upon applying the same set of rules that governs their family to their business?

The Family's Hierarchy Is the Business's Curse

Family businesses have a bad habit of wanting to transpose the hierarchy that exists within the family to the business. The most common example of this phenomenon is when roles in the company mirror the family's hierarchy—that is, people are assigned to jobs according to their birth order and often their sex.

Are the right people, then, in the right roles?

SOMETHING'S OUT OF ALIGNMENT

A car that's badly out of alignment is hard to steer. If ignored, the misalignment will destroy the front tires, producing a blowout that could cause the car to crash. Why should misalignment in a family business be any different?

What the business needs. A business needs to determine the most effective way to serve its marketplace. To do this, it must define how it will organize itself. The key objective in creating an organizational structure is establishing roles that best enable the business to serve the marketplace. Jobs are defined, including the number of people required to do the work, the specific tasks each job performs, and so on.

To be effective, each job requires a person with a certain set of skills and abilities. Therefore, the next step is to seek out and place people with the correct mix of skills and abilities into those jobs. It's like a football team: you put the really big kids on the line to block and send the really fast ones out for passes. Why should people think the family hierarchy mirrors the requirements of the jobs within their business?

What the business gets. Unfortunately, in a family business, the staffing of key assignments is usually a matter of birth order. The most senior management position available goes to the oldest child (or son), the second most important management position goes to the next oldest child (or son), and so on. It's common for female family members to be relegated to secondary roles within the business. The actual talents and abilities of the family members have no relationship to their business roles, often producing a management team that is unbelievably misaligned to handle the business's challenges.

Figure 5 presents a commonly encountered family-business organizational structure.

What needs to be done. The family must abandon the tradition of putting its members into positions within the family business according to birth order and other arbitrary criteria. Instead, they must recognize that this is a business and that the needs of the business take precedence over the family hierarchy and traditions.

But what happens when the family members—regardless of hierarchy—simply do not possess the skills or abilities required of the job positions that have been defined for the business? Good business sense would dictate that the family search for candidates outside of the family system and fill the jobs with those outsiders.

The family needs to step back and take a critical look at the skills and talents of its family members vis-à-vis the jobs available in its business. If family members do not possess the talents needed for a certain job and are not capable of growing into it, the family owes it to itself to fill that job with someone from outside the family.

FIGURE 5

The Family Hierarchy as Business Structure

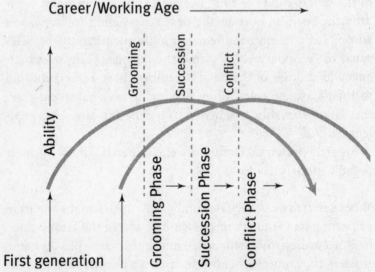

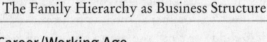

THE PAIN OF REARRANGING THE HIERARCHY

Imposing the family hierarchy onto the business structure is a great way to avoid having to make unpleasant decisions. After all, family members have accepted the hierarchical structure within their family system, so they'll probably do the same when the time comes to work in the business. Placing younger sons in charge of older ones, putting a daughter in charge, or telling certain children they're not qualified to work in the business is a prospect many families would rather not face.

Even if the parents try to apply best business practices and the business roles for the children are based on merit, this family-baggage pattern can be so strong that conflict arises among the children, who refuse to accept the fact that other brothers or sisters are being given greater authority or, worse yet, that they themselves are not qualified.

THE EFFECT(S) OF THIS BEHAVIOR PATTERN

In this behavior pattern the talent and ability of the family members are not linked to the business's role requirements, and there's no guarantee that their skills match the requirements of each job. Most likely, people have been stuck into the wrong jobs. They suffer, and the business suffers too.

"I Love All My Children Equally"

Good parents work hard to make sure that all their children feel equally loved. This staple of a healthy family system can create all kinds of problems if applied to the business system.

In some family businesses, it doesn't matter what the kids do—even if one works really hard and contributes to the business's success and the other is a total screwup. No, by God, these parents are determined that they're going to love all their children equally, and to prove it they're going to reward all of them equally.

EQUAL REWARDS FOR UNEQUAL WORK?

On the face of it, this proposition just won't work, yet many family businesses insist upon rewarding all their children equally, regardless of what they actually do.

When everyone gives their all. There are businesses in which all family members—parents and children alike—have dedicated themselves to the business and all have worked as hard as they can. In such a situation, parents often feel compelled to give everyone equal rewards.

I don't have problems with giving everyone equal rewards in such a situation; in fact, it's the fair thing to do. The problem I do have is that this scenario doesn't generally happen; it's rare for everyone in the family to have given their all.

When some work hard while others loaf. The most common scenario for a family that's fully employed in its business is that some members work hard while others loaf. So what do parents who love all their children equally do? Why, naturally, they continue to love all of their children equally and give everyone equal rewards. Here's where the trouble starts.

Even if the parents refuse to see it, the kids are very aware that they're making unequal sacrifices. While my heart goes out to the kids who are working the hardest, my admiration goes out to the loafers. Why not? The loafers have figured out how to maximize their benefits in their family's dysfunctional pattern. Only a martyr would work his or her butt off when he or she could receive an identical reward for just sitting on it.

Resentment galore. Over time, the resentment of the hard-working kids will grow. They'll be resentful toward their loafing siblings and, if they're healthy enough, at their parents for allowing this to happen. In the long run, this resentment will manifest itself in several ways.

First, it will demoralize the hardworking children, and demoralization zaps one's energy and clouds one's judgment. To keep the business viable, they must continue to solve problems energetically and seize opportunities. But at what point do demoralization and resentment convert into a desire to sabotage the business?

Second, the parents are setting the stage for all-out warfare among their children, which will inevitably occur as soon as the parents withdraw from the business and are no longer able to impose a truce.

REDEFINE "EQUALITY"

Parents have to teach their children that the family's business is not the same as the family, and that being loved equally within the family does not guarantee receiving an equal reward from the business. While equal love in a healthy family should be automatic and unconditional, equal love in the family's business means giving all members equal opportunities to make their maximum contributions.

THE DANGER OF LOVING ALL CHILDREN EQUALLY IN SUCCESSION

Some people mistakenly believe that the ultimate way for parents to demonstrate their equal love for their children is to give all of their children equal ownership in the business. The destructiveness of this institutionalized form of equal love is covered fully in Chapter 17.

Don't do it. This institutionalizes in perpetuity the source of ongoing resentment between the hard workers and the loafers.

THE EFFECT(S) OF THIS BEHAVIOR PATTERN

There are two detrimental effects of loving all your children equally in the business. First, it fosters resentment. Some people contribute to the success of the business while others do nothing, yet all receive equal rewards. Second, succession conducted in this manner grants equal amounts of ownership and control to people who have no interest in the business, who have no talent for it, or who have other priorities. All these effects will only foster conflict.

"Peace in Our Time"

Some family members value harmony above all else and will do anything to avoid conflict. This frequently occurs in families with deep-seated, serious conflicts. The harmony that is so highly valued indicates not a healthy family but rather the lack of open warfare. They can convince themselves that everyone's happy so long as no one's fighting.

SO YOU FEEL VULNERABLE

In most families, someone takes on the role of the family peacekeeper. Often the mother just wants everyone to be nice and get along. Can we expect different behavior from these family peacekeepers when they're working in the family business?

The main reason one family member takes on the role of family peacekeeper is that he or she feels quite vulnerable. There are numerous reasons for these feelings of vulnerability, be it something specific such as the recent death or disability of a spouse or just a general feeling of weakness vis-à-vis the other family members. The key thing to recognize is that this feeling of vulnerability drives this behavior pattern. When you perceive vulnerability in someone, look for this syndrome. The only way these family peacekeepers know how to lessen their feelings of vulnerability is by maintaining the family's harmony, which becomes their paramount objective in the business.

APPEASEMENT 101

Family peacekeepers primarily use two techniques to try to maintain the family harmony in the family's business.

Don't address it. Family peacekeepers refuse to allow difficult or sensitive issues to be addressed. It doesn't matter what's written in their job description—assuming that the business even has written job descriptions, which is seldom the case—these peacekeepers somehow believe that their one and only job in the family business is to prevent these issues from being addressed. Unfortunately, I can't think of any topics of substance or importance within a business that aren't fraught with difficult or sensitive issues. For example, there are key strategic planning issues such as what the product offerings should be, which markets should be served, what customer preferences are; critical staff issues such as addressing poor performance among employees; or the granddaddy of them all, succession issues, such as who will get control, what the form of ownership will be, and so on. Each of these issues is open to varying viewpoints and interpretations. There's no way to be in business and not have to deal with sensitive, difficult, and even potentially painful issues.

Ironically, sometimes the reason family peacekeepers feel insecure is that there seem to be long-running, deep-seated conflicts among family members. But in many cases, the deep-seated conflicts that continually arise are nothing more than the product of the family's consistently failing to address these difficult issues. The conflicts will never go away because the underlying issues causing them are never addressed, and time merely acts to irritate, exacerbate, and amplify them.

When in doubt, they placate. Family peacekeepers make decisions or take action with the sole intent of keeping the peace. Nowhere in this equation is there a notion of getting at and resolving the underlying root cause of a problem; therefore, these decisions or actions are often at conflict with the business's best interests. A great example of this peacekeeper behavior occurs when assigning family members jobs. The family peacekeeper will decide job appointments with the sole intent of appeasing family members' personal wishes rather than based on an honest evaluation of their merits or abilities. As a result, the business will have a group of placated family employees who are incompetent to do the task.

THE EFFECT(S) OF THIS BEHAVIOR PATTERN

The effect of playing peacekeeper—deferring tough issues or taking actions intended to placate people—is to continually defer conflicts when they arise. The conflict is not merely deferred, it grows and intensifies, making its resolution more difficult. If left unresolved long enough, conflicts that would have been troublesome to resolve will now be fatal to the business.

Shuttle Diplomacy Bogged Down by Baggage

Another dysfunctional family pattern that finds its way into businesses is the "triangling" phenomenon. In triangling, one family member uses a third person to serve as an intermediary, ally, or buffer in their interactions with a second family member rather than interacting directly with that second person.

While not desirable, there are times when this behavior pattern is acceptable within the family system. Problems within the family are not always urgent; they can resolve themselves slowly. Also, anger among family members may be intense and family members can't always flee one another, so maybe this is a reasonable way to make the best of a bad situation.

But this same behavior among family members working in the business brings with it a set of problems.

DRAWBACKS TO USING THIRD-PARTY INTERMEDIARIES

The business needs to get its problems solved. Communicating via an intermediary takes longer and consumes more energy. At a minimum, the amount of labor that will be spent facilitating a communication is doubled. I know of few businesses that can routinely waste this kind of energy. Unlike in the family, the delays involved in solving problems create lost profits. Lose enough profits, and you'll be out of business.

Transmission errors. Communication inevitably becomes garbled as it passes through an intermediary, especially one lacking strong interpersonal skills. This is best illustrated by the children's game of "telephone," where people sit in a circle and pass a verbal message around the circle. By the time the message travels full circle and returns to the originator, it seldom bears any resemblance to the original message. It's hard enough for two people having a conversation not to filter what they hear; this problem is compounded when a third party is utilized to relay messages.

The Balkan scenario. Europeans are frightened of wars in the Balkans because they have a nasty habit of dragging the rest of Europe into the conflict. The same happens when intermediaries are used to relay messages in the family business.

The selection of an intermediary indicates trust in the individual by the party who selected him or her. But the intermediary may easily be misconstrued as someone's ally and end up being blamed for taking sides even though he or she didn't.

There are two things family members need to remember before deciding to choose someone to play the role of a shuttle diplomat. First is the issue of whether these people have the power to say "no," especially if they're an employee rather than a family member. Second, people need to be left alone to do their jobs. Remember, they're employed because the business needs certain things done, and they can't do what they're supposed to be doing if they're wasting time shuttling the family's baggage.

What about the real problem? An intermediary is being used because there's a problem between two family members who will not talk. Unless the third party is a trained therapist, using an intermediary often guarantees that the two people with the problem will never directly confront each other and thereby get at the root cause of the problem. How long can a business afford to keep spending money to prop up this problem?

SO YOU THINK YOU'RE ANOTHER HENRY KISSINGER?

Using third-party intermediaries to avoid direct communication among family members is akin to using shuttle diplomacy. It resurrects images of Henry Kissinger shuttling back and forth among countries at war. But is this any way to run a business?

What elements combine to make for a successful shuttle diplomat? First and foremost, they're not weighted down in their journeys by having to carry the family's baggage.

A higher purpose. Shuttle diplomats must be seen as being impartial. Moreover, they are seen as having a duty to something greater than merely relaying messages in order to avoid the immediate conflict. They must be perceived as placing the best interests of the family business above the personal interests of any individual parties.

An outsider. Effective shuttle diplomats must be able to walk away from the current situation. They cannot be dependent upon a continuing job in the business or upon continuing to stay within the family system.

A rare combination of talents. Henry Kissinger had rare talents that combined to give him a powerful presence. He was a major figure on the international scene and a key member of a powerful government. He had a healthy ego that gave him the ability to assert himself when confronting other people. Finally, he had a tremendous intellect. How many people can you find within a family business who have this combination of traits?

Family businesses need to ask themselves two questions. First, do they really have someone with these kinds of abilities working in the business? Second, if they do, why the heck are these people taking orders from the family? Shouldn't they be in charge of the family business and the family taking instructions from them?

It's in their job description. Let's not forget, Henry Kissinger's job was to involve himself in major international crises. It's what he was paid to do. Family businesses need to remember that their people are not employed to be shuttle diplomats. Rather, they're employed to do their jobs, which involve other tasks.

If you insist on using a shuttle diplomat, remember that the only people who do have this role in their job descriptions are outside business advisors.

THE EFFECT(S) OF THIS BEHAVIOR PATTERN

Three significant effects arise from resorting to shuttle diplomacy in a business. First, conflicts will inevitably worsen because a lot of energy is consumed without resolving the real issues. Second, unresolved conflicts tend to worsen over time. Third, the act of using an intermediary often sows the seeds of additional conflicts within the business, as the selection of an intermediary within the business may unwittingly promote rivalries and pit people against one another.

The "We're One Big Happy Family" Syndrome

Failure to acknowledge that the business system requires different practices than the family system.

Manifestation	Description	Effect(s)
The family's hierarchy is the business's curse	The family hierarchy is imposed onto the business.	People's abilities seldom match the requirements of their jobs—the wrong people are in the wrong jobs.
"I love all my children equally"	All children are rewarded equally, regardless of their contributions to the business's success/failure.	Fosters resentment among family members. Creates conflicting interests if ownership (i.e., control) is dispersed incorrectly.
"Peace in our time"	Harmony is paramount: it must be maintained by avoiding disagreements.	Critical issues are never addressed or resolved. Amplifies the intensity of conflicts when they inevitably arise.
Shuttle diplomacy bogged down by baggage	Using third parties to deliver "confrontational" messages.	Wastes time. Fosters additional conflicts by dragging third parties into the situation.

6

......

"They May Have Become Adults, but They'll Always Be My Children"

There's no automatic guarantee that children will be treated like adults as they get older. Their employment in the family business is certainly no guarantee of it either.

After All, They're the Ones Who Used to Change Your Diapers

One of the many problems with parents is that they remember you as an infant. Unfortunately, they have certain images of you indelibly burned into their memory. Some of these memories include having to change your diapers (including cleaning the poop off of your butt), hearing you crying out in the night because there was a monster under your bed, and other assorted adventures. So even though you have your Stanford MBA (those of us on the West Coast don't harbor the mistaken notion that Harvard has the best MBA), do you actually expect your parents to listen to anything you have to say when it comes to running their business? Get real.

AUTOMATIC NULLIFICATION

"Children should be seen and not heard." This saying takes on new dimensions when applied to a family business.

Ideas may be summarily dismissed. Adult children who have entered into their parents' business often bring a slew of new ideas and approaches with them. Tragically, the business doesn't benefit because the parents instinctively reject these new ideas.

I doubt that the parents are aware that they're doing this. The behavior is often so subtle that it's as though the kids never said anything and the parents didn't hear them. I attribute it to selective deafness, and it's its subtlety that makes it so exasperating for the kids. It would be easier if the parents would just say, "Shut up and go to your room." At least the kids could then confront their parents on the issue.

These same parents who don't listen to their kids' new ideas will bend over backward to listen to the ideas of the biggest idiot (as defined by the children) on their payroll. The effect is to add insult to injury to their kids.

Decisions may be countermanded. The parents' ability to nullify their adult children isn't limited to their kids' ideas; it also extends to their kids' business decisions.

Some parents will reflexively overrule business decisions made by their kids. It's as though if the kid decides "A," parents insist that the correct decision should be "B." They'd never think of doing this to any other employee, but the fact that it's their kid gives them license to intervene at will. Just about any other employee's decision would have been given the benefit of the doubt.

YOU EXPECT ME TO PUT THE KID WHO POOPED IN HIS DIAPERS IN CHARGE?

Parents may also unknowingly fail to accept their children as grown adults by failing to delegate them proper authority.

Officially. This is the most blatant form, where children are never given any formal decision-making authority in their jobs. Instead, they're allocated technical tasks or ceremonial roles—jobs that do not require decisions to be made. It doesn't matter what their title is, because any and all decisions are made by others, usually their parents. For example, in one company the adult son had the title Vice President of Sales. But rather than having the authority to approve the sales staff's price quotations, he had to first show them to his father, who would decide.

Unofficially. While the kids might technically have full decision-making authority in their jobs, it's still possible for their parents to unofficially fail to delegate sufficient authority to them. How is this possible? It happens when the children have learned to expect that their decisions will be countermanded or their ideas summarily dismissed. Though technically they do have the authority, as a practical matter they won't assert themselves, knowing that their parents will inevitably override their decisions.

THE EFFECT(S) OF THIS BEHAVIOR PATTERN

The business fails to get the benefit of the kids' ideas. In addition, it does not fully utilize their ability to make decisions and take on responsible tasks. On a personal level, this behavior creates feelings of exasperation and anger among the kids and may create or exacerbate conflicts.

"What Does It Say About Me If My Kids Are Middle-Aged?"

Family systems can be tenacious, and the ability to deny that the children are grown adults may continue indefinitely. Physically, the "kids" might have grown to be middle-aged adults, but their family system still defines them as children and forces this role onto them within the business system.

THERE'S MOUNTING EVIDENCE THAT YOU MIGHT NOT BE IMMORTAL

It's painful when evidence of one's own mortality comes from looking at your children. But what other conclusions are possible when you look at your children and see the following signs: they're starting to have gray hair (if they haven't lost it), they've been wearing Dockers for years, and their children are doing the same irritating things to them that they used to do to you. The conclusion is inescapable: you've become your grandparents, and grandparents eventually die.

Rather than accepting the inevitable, these parents are convinced that they can prevent the aging process through the power of sheer denial. If they can somehow keep their kids as "kids," they'll be prevented from aging. By golly, that's it: they won't allow their children to become grown-up adults.

IT'S EASY IF THEY NEVER LEFT AND CAME BACK

In many family businesses, the children moved directly into the business upon completing school (assuming they weren't already working there). In this situation, there was no clear event delineating the transition from childhood into adulthood. The sheer continuity of their presence in both the family and the business system serves to blur the fact that they've aged.

Contrast this with kids who went away to college and embarked upon careers outside the family business. They may have been away from the immediate family and living independent lives in another state for twenty years before returning to work in the family business. In this case, there was a distinct passage of time and a clear delineation between their childhood and their adulthood. Parents in these situations find it more difficult to deny these children's adulthood. What's more, the kids themselves won't stand for it.

WHAT DOES IT SAY ABOUT A FAMILY SYSTEM THAT SEEKS TO DENY REALITY?

If a predominant mind-set of the family system is a desire to deny reality, manifested in the parents' unwillingness to acknowledge their children as being grown-up adults, it's safe to assume that the same mind-set is projected into their business system. To what extent will the owners look out into the marketplace with a desire that things were the way they used to be rather than searching for new directions, trends, and opportunities?

Vis-à-vis the business. There's a danger that the owners will seek to maintain the status quo in how they run their business.

If they don't want their children to change, why should they want their business to change? They will be less willing to experiment and adopt new methods. While a certain amount of resistance to change is normal as people age, here it's exaggerated.

Vis-à-vis the family. Another critical issue is the extent to which the children have inherited their parents' penchant for denial. Remember, they're products of a family system that has emphasized denial. Therefore, being loyal to their family system means that they must also deny that they have become adults. Rather than growing into healthy, independent, assertive, high-functioning adults, they must stay in the role of children and be forever dependent upon their parents in order to prove their loyalty. It's a behavior pattern they may not be able to switch off once the parents have departed from the business. I know of a business where the parents have retired and moved to Florida, but the kids are continually on the phone asking for permission before they make decisions—sometimes making several calls in one day!

THE EFFECT(S) OF THIS BEHAVIOR PATTERN

First, there's an unusually strong desire to maintain the status quo within the business, hindering the business's ability to seize new opportunities. Second, there's the danger that the kids have learned to make themselves dependent upon their parents, undermining their ability to develop into competent adults capable of contributing to the business's success as well as potentially taking over as successors.

The Oedipus Complex: Reversed, Redefined, and Thoroughly Reengineered

The Oedipus complex refers to a psychoanalytical syndrome based on an ancient Greek drama in which the son feels compelled to kill his father in order to gain his freedom (and win his mother's affection, but that's way too Freudian for me). While the first part of the equation might be tempting, with the possible exception of the Menendez brothers this compulsion doesn't seem to have caught on. Or has it?

An argument can be made that the parents have been doing their homework and have found a way to reverse the Oedipus complex: they feel compelled to kill their children in order to retain their freedom. Since they can't legally do this, they've reengineered the concept to include suppressing their kids.

IT'S STILL ABOUT COMPETITION

People who start or run family businesses are often competitive by nature. While competitiveness is good in their business-system role, it can create significant problems when they bring this competitiveness into their family-system relationships.

Compete with your competitors, not with your family. First and foremost, your business is in competition, but it is in competition in the marketplace against all of your competitors. Effective business systems direct their competitive energies externally and promote cooperative energies inwardly.

Some families don't understand that there can be a number of adults within a family system. There's no need for the parents always to be the sole adult members of the family system; it's not a win-lose competition if other adults emerge within the family. If anything, it's in the family's best interest to make competent adults of their children, especially if they're going to be brought into the family business.

Most of your competitors are actively developing the managerial and technical skills of their employees. Metaphorically speaking, they are developing their staffs into a cadre of healthy adults. If you're going to go into battle against these other businesses, you need to be doing the same with your children.

They're past their prime. If the children are grown-up adults, it's probably safe to assume that the parents have passed their physical prime. If nothing else, the sheer ordeal of raising children is enough to almost destroy one's mind and body. Running a business is also challenging physically, emotionally, and intellectually, and if they've been doing it for years, aren't they beginning to get tired? Are their interest and passion still there?

Just like professional athletes, there comes a time when the parents will no longer be in the prime of their game and the abilities of their grown children will exceed theirs. The truth about many professional athletes is that they're still able to outplay almost anyone else even thirty-plus years after retirement; they're just not able to compete against professional athletes from younger generations. Business owners are no different.

TECHNIQUES TO SABOTAGE THE KIDS

Since children have a pesky habit of growing up to be adults, it sometimes becomes necessary to employ techniques designed to inhibit their development. These techniques attempt to delay the inevitable.

Don't develop them. The more the children learn about the business, strengthen key skills, and develop their talents, the more "adultlike" they become. The key, then, is not to let this happen.

Parents in competition with their children avoid giving their children jobs and assignments that have the potential to help develop competent successors. Instead they will put them into jobs where they perform narrowly defined technical tasks. This can always be disguised as "You need to master the fundamentals," but a warning sign arises when the children are not periodically rotated to different positions to learn new skills. In one distribution company, the son was forced to work in the warehouse for the first ten years. Since then, he's spent almost a decade in dispatch. As his fortieth birthday approaches, it appears that he might be ready to begin to handle minor bookkeeping tasks. He has never participated in a management meeting—he's not yet ready because he doesn't have the background!

Overwhelm them into submission. What better way to keep children from asserting themselves as competent adults than to make sure they fail at something—and miserably! (And people think that breaking wild horses is a lost vocation.) The trick is to give them a job or assignment that they can't possibly handle, one that requires a series of skills they haven't yet mastered and complex knowledge they do not possess.

An advantage of this practice, from the parents' perspective, is that it allows them to conclusively state "You're not ready" should that child begin to reassert him- or herself. In fact, if the failure is particularly traumatic, it may have the added benefit of stifling all the siblings. The parents need pull off this trick only once. All they need to do in the future to validate their "You're not ready" contention is to refer back to this episode.

The danger to the business from this practice is both immediate and long term. It's expensive to arrange for a failure; you have to pay salaries while the damage is being done, and also for the costs of undoing any mistakes. A failure can harm the child's self-confidence and self-esteem, hampering his or her job performance. In the long run, this episode may cause lingering doubts about his or her eventual ability to handle any critical assignments or even possibly head the family's business (or any other business for that matter, should he or she want to go elsewhere).

LET'S PIT BILLY AGAINST BOBBY

As a final act of desperation, parents in competition with their children actively promote rivalries among them. You'll note that I've used the word "rivalries," not "competition." This practice is usually reserved for significantly dysfunctional family systems.

If they are successful, the kids will be so busy fighting with one another that they will make no attempt to take on adult roles within the business. Having the kids at one another's throats serves to validate the parents' need to remain in control of the business: "The kids can't do it—they're too busy misbehaving."

THE EFFECT(S) OF THIS BEHAVIOR PATTERN

Viewing children as competitors converts a child's ability to feel like a competent, healthy adult within the family's business into a win-lose contest, and the parents do not intend to lose. It is dangerous for the business, as the parents will remain in control past their prime. In addition, they will effectively have crippled would-be successors among their family, further weakening the long-run viability of the business.

The "They May Have Become Adults, but They'll Always Be My Children" Syndrome

Parents unable to accept their children as grown adults.

Manifestation	Description	Effect(s)
After all, they're the ones who used to change your diapers	Parents automatically reject children's new ideas and approaches; fail to delegate authority to them.	Children become angry and exasperated; the business is automatically denied potential contributions from them.
"What does it say about me if my kids are middle-aged?"	Parents deny that their children have become adults to avoid having to confront their own mortality.	Instinctive desire to maintain the status quo and see things in the past tense; increased resistance to change; children remain dependent rather than grow into independent contributors.
The oedipus complex: reversed, redefined, and thoroughly reengineered	Parents in competition with their children.	Parents remain in control of the business past their competitive prime; prospective successors are sabotaged and eliminated.

7

......

"You're Not Loyal to This Family If You Insist on Being Selfish"

When a rigid family system combines with dominating parents—look out! The result will be parents who project their feelings and desires onto their children. The children *must* think, feel, and believe the same way the parents do in everything. In order to be loyal members of the family, the children must be as passionate about the family business as their parents are.

Forget about the implications for family life; is this an effective formula for staffing the family business?

"There's Always Been a Starkadder at Cold Comfort Farm"

There is a delightful movie entitled *Cold Comfort Farm*. It's the story of a dysfunctional family's antics on a farm where the only crop growing is something called family baggage. Every time a family member wants to escape the farm and pursue his or her dreams, the family matriarch calls a family meeting, descends from the attic, and declares, "There's always been a

Starkadder at Cold Comfort Farm ... always has been ... always will be ..." No one leaves, and everyone is miserable.

This scenario is reenacted in family businesses everywhere, with tragic consequences for family members and their businesses. It's time for Starkadders everywhere to flee Cold Comfort Farm.

WHY DO YOU WANT TO CONDEMN YOUR CHILDREN TO BE LIKE YOU?

When parents force their children to be interested in the family business—as well as forcing their beliefs on just about everything else on them—they stifle their children's ability to define themselves. As a result, the children are never able to explore their talents, understand what they are best at, and thereby achieve their full potential.

You get better odds in Vegas. Some parts of people's identity—their personality, interests, traits, physical attributes—are genetically predetermined; others develop in response to environmental factors. We may never know which of these two factors is the most powerful, but what we do know is that the interplay of genetics and environment makes each person unique. And if people are unique, why is it that some family systems seem intent upon forcing all their members to be the same?

Because people are unique, each person is predisposed toward a specific role (i.e., job, career) at which he or she will excel. Conversely, it also means that there are other roles for which he or she is not well suited. But since there's such a diverse range of possibilities for how people can be predisposed, what are the odds that their true calling matches the role they are expected to assume in the family business?

The fact that people are related by blood doesn't guarantee

that they'll excel at working in the family business. That only works with racehorses. Has the family taken a person who might have been the next great Nobel laureate and instead cloned a younger version of Ma and Pa?

Do the children possess the right skills for the business? Let's not forget that the family business has a certain set of needs. Forcing the children to conform to a predetermined mold—how to think, how to feel, what their "talents" are—and then requiring them to go into the family business violates the business practice of first defining the roles needed by the business, then identifying the skills required to perform these roles, and finally identifying people possessing these skills, who will be given jobs. The odds are slim that parents looking only within the family will employ the right group of people.

THE CHILDREN'S MOTIVATION IS ALL WRONG

People's motivation—their reasons for doing something—can be a critical determining factor in whether they will be successful. There's no way of knowing in advance whether it will be a factor, but in situations where motivation does become relevant, it becomes critical.

Is the motivation internal or external? A person's motivation for doing something can be either internally or externally imposed, and this is a crucial distinction. When you ask someone his or her motivation for doing something, he or she can usually give you a pretty good explanation. The important thing to remember is that even though the words are coming out of their mouth and sound like their own words, few people have sufficient self-awareness to truly understand whether their motivation is internally imposed (i.e., it's something they want to do) or has been externally imposed upon them (i.e., they're doing what they're doing to try to please someone else, sometimes unknowingly). It's sad when people trick themselves into believing that an externally imposed motivation is internally imposed.

Internally imposed motivation comes about through a process of self-definition. Internally motivated people take the time, spend the energy, and ask themselves who they are and what their talents are, thereby defining what it is they really want to do. Such people are rare. Their motivation is converted into passion—a consuming passion that propels them to do what they're doing.

Externally imposed motivation is akin to a sense of obligation. Rather than searching for self-definition, people with this sort of motivation have decided to conform to their family's system. But since they don't know themselves, they don't know that this isn't what they really want to do. Lacking the passion to pursue their true destiny, they're just going through the motions—and they're doing so in the family business.

Let's hope all is smooth sailing. So why my emphasis on passion in the preceding paragraphs? It's because passion may be the vital element needed when things go wrong with the family business.

Remember, if the motivation has been externally imposed, the children are complying with a role that has been forced upon them through a sense of obligation. While they may be technically competent in their jobs, they have no inner resolve to sustain them through setbacks or difficult periods. These are people who allow themselves to be overwhelmed when business difficulties arise.

THEIR HEART IS SOMEPLACE ELSE

So what's the reward of failing to acknowledge family members as individuals with talents lying outside those needed for the family business?

Lack of commitment. Prisoners might show respect to their guards by addressing them as "sir," but do you think they really mean it? A family may confuse "being committed" (according to *The Random House Dictionary,* "possessing strong desire and determination to achieve success") with "being committed" ("to place in confinement or custody").

How can these children be passionate about the business when the family has imposed a role on them that usually bears no relation to their talents? They will probably do an adequate job and the business will likely continue, but it will not achieve the potential it could have with a group of highly motivated employees.

The saboteurs among us. The children who have managed to trick themselves into believing that their externally imposed motivation is really their own are the ones who lack commitment. But there's another group of children, those who know they're not where they want to be—and they're resentful.

The danger of having resentful children working in the family's business is that they often harbor an unconscious desire to sabotage the business. Remember, the family system is not healthy, so these children can't be expected to assert themselves in a rational or appropriate manner. They won't suddenly assert their individuality and walk away from the business (and possibly from the family itself) to pursue their true calling. Instead, the only way they know how to get even with having been forced into their role is to eliminate the role itself, and since the family probably won't or can't eliminate the role, the only way out is to destroy the company. I've seen numerous instances where such children begin to quietly undermine the business's performance—commitments to key customers aren't met, production deadlines pass, or things simply fall through the cracks. Their actions are never obvious—except to an outside observer.

THE EFFECT(S) OF THIS BEHAVIOR PATTERN

Parents create a family group of employees who are closer to being prisoners of the business than they are to being committed entrepreneurs. At best, the business will have employees who aren't able to perform as well as a truly committed, passionate group of employees; at worst, a group of saboteurs is lying in wait.

Sitting in the Back of the Family Bus

Children who do assert their individuality against a family system that demands conformity will be forced to pay a price for their actions, and they will not be treated as equals within the family.

A DYSFUNCTIONAL FAMILY = EXCOMMUNICATION

Dysfunctional families are incapable of separating the family and the business systems. Such families will respond to their children's decision to remove themselves from the business system by throwing them out of the family system too.

Individuality is viewed as betrayal. Among other problems, these families are riddled with boundary issues. People don't understand where their identity ends and others' begins.

Let's start with the parents. Remember, the parents will not allow their children to be individuals; instead, they must be absolute reflections of the parents. A child's individuality is interpreted as a personal betrayal of the parents.

How about the siblings? Nope, children asserting themselves as individuals can't expect much better treatment from their siblings. Remember, the ones who decide to stay within the system (as though they have a choice) are forced to agree with their parents. And if they want to succeed rather than merely survive within their family, they must trick themselves into believing that their parents' wishes are their own; therefore, they take the attitude that the person who wants to leave the business is also betraying them personally. Even if they don't, there's bound to be some resentment since they've conformed to the system and are suffering because of it, so why shouldn't everyone?

I know of a family who owns a bank. Rather than join his brothers at the bank, the middle son moved to the East Coast to play in a symphony. The brothers haven't spoken to their wayward brother in years because they believe he's "playing" with his musical instrument—real work is something that is done in an office. They're also angry that their brother seems to love what he's doing: "We're not having fun at the bank; he shouldn't be able to either."

Maybe the Domino Theory is real and there are Communists hiding under your bed. Early in the Cold War, Americans believed in the Domino Theory—they feared that if a single country became Communist, the ones around it would also, one after the other. Anything un-American was evil, people were pressured to conform, and those who didn't could be ostracized for not being American enough.

These family systems contain their own version of the Domino Theory. People who do not conform by working in the family's business are viewed as being evil because they are unfamily, and ostracizing them serves to unite the family and reinforce the system. Any child asserting his or her individuality and departing from the family business is excommunicated from the family to prevent him or her from contaminating others. This family fears that if one person decides not to conform, others will follow.

A NORMAL FAMILY = SECOND-CLASS CITIZENSHIP

The preceding section paints a bleak picture. I wish it were fiction. There are, however, families who actually encourage and support their children to do their own thing. These families accept "individuals" as full members of the family system.

Unfortunately, even in these family systems children who work outside the family business may become de facto second-class citizens. This is neither deliberate nor intentional; rather, it's a natural consequence of certain circumstances.

Out of sight, out of mind. All else being equal, when a person is employed outside the family business, this person just isn't around as much as the other family members. After all, the family members working together are probably tripping over one another all day long.

Children who pursue their own interests may also have moved to another town. Contact with them and the rest of the family may be limited to occasional phone calls and holiday visits, whereas even if the family business has geographically dispersed offices and its members live in different towns, they're still regularly in touch with one another on business matters.

Relating to one another via dual systems. All family members relate to one another in their family roles regardless of how often they see one another or where they work. But family members who work together find that they have another dimension on which they can relate. All face the common issues, antics, and problems that occur within the family business. They're not just family members; they're also coworkers.

Children pursuing their own interests are employed elsewhere. As such, they and their family members will never be able to relate to each other as coworkers. There's also the possibility that the family may not be able to understand what the children do for a living since their vocation probably bears no resemblance to the family business.

THE EFFECT(S) OF THIS BEHAVIOR PATTERN

Requiring conformity and forcing family members into the family business creates serious conflict between family members who want to work elsewhere and the rest of the family. Even in families that encourage children to do their own thing, the children who don't work in the family business are not quite as equal as those who do, providing a potential source of conflict.

The "You're Not Loyal to This Family If You Insist on Being Selfish" Syndrome

Failure to acknowledge family members as individuals.

Manifestation	Description	Effect(s)
"There's always been a Starkadder at Cold Comfort Farm"	Children are expected to want to go into the family's business.	Children's self-definition is stifled, creating resentment and a potential desire to sabotage the business or a lack of full commitment to it.
Sitting in the back of the family bus	Family members not participating in the business become second-class citizens.	Creates alienation and estrangement between family members; provides defacto rationale for conflict.

8

......

Father Knows Best?

Two relatively safe generalizations can be made about people who start businesses: they usually have a domineering personality, and they are consumed by their business. These traits have ramifications for the family system that spill over into the business system.

"Who Are You?"

Business founders (and the head of any family business for that matter) may become so consumed with running their business that it becomes their life. We're not talking about someone who works hard; we're talking about a workaholic. Family members are relegated to a status of lesser importance than the business.

I KNOW I HAVE A DAD (OR HUSBAND) BECAUSE HIS MAIL IS DELIVERED HERE

People consumed with running their business lack the ability to spend a lot of time with their families. They may be designated "absentee family members"—absentee parent or absentee spouse. This chapter is titled "Father Knows Best?"; but the term may also apply to mothers or to both parents. The fact that a parent does not spend sufficient time and energy with the family may create a series of issues.

Who has time for this relationship stuff? Absentee family members often fail to develop a meaningful relationship with their children as well as with their spouses.

Think about it: Developing and then maintaining a meaningful relationship requires significant time and energy. It's not something that can be accomplished by dabbling. People who are overly consumed with running their business simply do not have the requisite time and energy.

One of the social myths that emerged in the 1980s was the notion of a "Superwoman"—one who was able to simultaneously be both a superstar career woman and a great parent. That's nonsense—it just doesn't happen because of the trade-offs that occur. Let's flip this around and apply it to the Father Knows Best? syndrome. It is possible to successfully start a business and be a successful parent, but it's not possible in the Father Knows Best? syndrome because what we're talking about here are people who are consumed with their business to the exclusion of everything else.

Family members will eventually come to recognize that the business is far more important to the absentee family member than they are, since time was never set aside to develop and maintain familial relationships.

What needs could they have? I'm a good provider. Absentee fathers are often oblivious to their family's psychological needs. These needs include parental approval or validation, emotional intimacy, or having a parent or spouse to share significant experiences with.

Absentee fathers have the mistaken notion that they are providing these needs as long as they periodically show up for key events. But the truth is that they can't fulfill these needs if they haven't taken the time to get to know their family. Interactions with family members become nothing more than an entry in an appointment book.

DIFFERING PERSPECTIVES ON THE SAME MATTER

It's interesting how absentee fathers and their families have differing perspectives on this situation.

"I did it for you!" We'll begin with the perspective of the father who knows best.

Let's start by cutting through the crap. You didn't do it for them, you did it for yourself—and that's okay. There's nothing wrong with that as long as you have the decency to be honest and admit it. I've found that in many cases the feelings of alienation and estrangement don't stem from the fact that the absentee father is consumed with the business. Rather, it's the failure to be honest about *why* they did what they did that creates problems.

People fully consumed with their business are meeting their own needs—whatever they may be. There are probably demons deep within their psyche driving them. If your spouse expects you to kill yourself to provide for her lifestyle, the question is: Why did you marry her? If your children have similar expectations, the question is: Why did you let them get spoiled? In either scenario, you claim that others force you to do what you do, but the motivation must be coming from someplace inside you yourself.

Disingenuous statements by absentee family members can cause great pain. It's not the fact that they're absent, it's their insistence that the other family members are more important than they really are that causes the problems.

"Where were you?" Now for the perspective of the kids—and sometimes the spouse.

Your kids have friends whose fathers probably did seemingly inconsequential things with them. Things like showing them how to play ball, participating in scouting, or showing up for back-to-school night. Your kids can't be expected to understand the obligations of founding or running a business. All they see is that you're not there.

What is most valued by your family is not the economic benefits your business brings them. Instead, they want to see more of you, to do little things with you, especially if they did not ask you to consume yourself with the business on their behalf.

THE EFFECT(S) OF THIS BEHAVIOR PATTERN

The most immediate effect of this behavior is alienation within the family system, coupled with resentment toward the absentee parent for failing to be honest. If the absentee father is able to keep the family out of the business, the impact on the business system will probably be minimal. But if other family members do become involved in the business, their work will be tainted by these negative emotions.

Nonpersons

A common trait among entrepreneurs is a domineering presence and a strong need to control. These traits may contribute to their success in business, but they may also create dysfunctional families.

If entrepreneurs intend to bring their children into the business, there's going to be trouble. Interacting with children in a controlling manner does not produce healthy, competent adults—it produces nonpersons. Physically they're no longer children, but they can't be categorized as adults either.

YOU NEED COMPETENT CHILDREN, NOT NONPERSONS, IN YOUR BUSINESS

Domination and control within the family system stifles the development of children who are slated to go into the family business. Problems will eventually arise since these children will bring unresolved issues and conflicts into adulthood, and subsequently into the family business.

Consultants and other advisors need to be particularly aware of this phenomenon and the corresponding issues anytime they're working with a family business where there's an entrepreneur in the picture.

These children lack decision-making skills. Because these nonpersons have been dominated and controlled all their lives, it's doubtful that they've had an opportunity to make many decisions for themselves, especially in a business context. So how good can their decision-making skills be? Even assuming they are reasonably good, *will* they make decisions? Probably not, as long as the specter of their domineering parent remains somewhere in their mind. They've had a lifetime of experiences that have taught them that making independent decisions is not worth the penalty they'll incur.

They lack self-confidence. These children have probably spent much of their energy trying to minimize the painful impact of being controlled. The easiest route is often compliance. But if they have grown into adulthood complying, how can they understand who and what they really are?

Part of developing self-confidence is knowing oneself. These children haven't had the opportunity to discover themselves, so they will lack the self-confidence required to be effective contributors to the business.

They're either Jekyll or Hyde managers. It's doubtful that these nonpersons will be effective managers, because their parent has been their role model. And because they're bringing unresolved issues with that parent into the business, they often adopt one of two extreme managerial styles.

The first is to mimic the controlling style used by their parent. They've had ample opportunity to observe this style, and it has been used in the business before.

The second is not to be like their parent; instead, the nonperson will be overly accommodating. He or she will try to be the kind, understanding parent he or she never had.

In fact, the optimum style is somewhere in between.

HAS THE FATHER WHO KNOWS BEST GUARANTEED THAT HE'LL ALWAYS BE IN CONTROL?

In the absence of interventions such as using outside advisors to introduce new ways of acting or sending nonpersons to training courses to learn new skills, nonpersons can expect to be nonpersons indefinitely.

Can the entrepreneur give up control? If the reason for the nonperson being a nonperson is the presence of a controlling parent, all that's needed to fix the situation is the departure of that parent from the business. Right? Don't count on it.

It is not realistic to expect a controlling owner to give up control of their business. They need control and their business has been providing a steady source for years. It's akin to expecting a junkie to quit an addiction. Entrepreneurs believe that success has come because they have been in control. To share authority with their adult children is to give up direct control. They're being asked to give up the very thing that made the success possible.

Can nonpersons assert themselves and take charge? Don't expect the nonpersons to begin asserting themselves as they enter the business. After all, they've learned to survive a controlling parent by submitting, and *it is* their parent's company. Why fight it? It's unrealistic to expect them to suddenly change.

Even if he dies, he's still there. When nonpersons have been identified as eventual successors, the business is vulnerable. Controlling entrepreneurs create a business that is dependent on their presence. By creating nonpersons, the owner creates a group of would-be successors who are incapable of stepping in and taking over the business should the entrepreneur decide to retire. As these nonpersons inevitably flounder, the entrepreneur will be compelled to reenter the business. It's a way of never having to give up control.

What if the entrepreneur should suddenly pass away? Though physically removed from both the family system and the business system, the entrepreneur's spirit remains. Nonpersons are not going to immediately undo a lifetime of learned behavior patterns and rise to the occasion. I've worked with only one company that went bankrupt, and the bankruptcy had nothing to do with running out of money. Dad was a Type A entrepreneur who dropped dead standing next to his desk.

His sons could not step up and take control—they couldn't make a single decision. When I was called in four months later, all that could be done with this once successful business was to file for bankruptcy.

THE EFFECT(S) OF THIS BEHAVIOR PATTERN

The business is unable to continue without the presence of the entrepreneur's control (in the absence of significant outside intervention via consultants and advisors) because the business has been taught to rely on the entrepreneur's control and potential successors have failed to learn how to assert themselves, are lacking in self-confidence, and possess questionable managerial skills.

"It's MY Company"

A funny thing happens with people who possess a domineering personality and who are totally consumed with their business. After a while, the boundaries between themselves and their business begin to blur. Eventually, they may begin to view the company as an extension of their own identity. They and their business have become one.

"MINE! MINE! ALL MINE!"

Entrepreneurs may become possessive of *their* company. Like children who don't want anyone else playing with their toys, they begin to lash out at other family members who get involved in it. It's an interesting paradox: on the one hand, they might have forced them to work in the business, but once they're there, the entrepreneur keeps such tight control over them that they can be only marginally effective.

Should the other family members begin to be successful, they'll be viewed as a threat. Remember, this owner wants to be in control, and that owner *is* the company. Someone else's successful performance threatens his need to have absolute control. No one likes it when other kids play with their toys better than they can. As a result, the owner will seek to undermine whichever family member is threatening.

In one company, the father took pride in being the top salesman. His son joined him in the business and soon began to excel at sales. Because the father felt threatened by this son's success in *his* company, he continually reassigned the son to new sales territories to ensure that *he* (Dad) would always be the top salesman at *his* company.

UNGRATEFUL LITTLE . . .

Entrepreneurs and business founders may feel resentful toward their children, whom they view as eventual inheritors to the business who didn't work hard to create it. Their feeling is "I did all the work to build my business, and my children are going to inherit this windfall."

They're caught in a quandary. Should they leave their business to their children or not? The latter is a tempting but unpleasant option. And there will be hell to pay from the family if they cut their children out of their will. This quandary helps reinforce their feelings of resentment.

THE EFFECT(S) OF THIS BEHAVIOR PATTERN

The owner either fails to support or seeks to undermine family members who involve themselves in *their* company.

The Father Knows Best? Syndrome

Business founders usually possess dominating personalities and/or are consumed with the business.

Manifestation	Description	Effect(s)
"Who are you?"	Business founders are consumed with running their business to the exclusion of everything else.	Alienation and estrangement arise between founders and their family.
Nonpersons	Business founders with dominating personalities or a strong need to control interact with family members in this manner.	The children grow into adults being unable to assert themselves; the business becomes dependent upon the continued presence of the founder.
"It's MY company"	Business founders view the company as an extension of their own identity.	Founders become possessive of "their" company; undermining family members who participate in the business; feel resentful toward inheritors.

9

......

"Maybe It Will Go Away If We Ignore It"

Some problems only get worse over time. Situations that would have been minor inconveniences had they been addressed immediately can eventually become bad enough to kill a business.

Many families have a pattern of deferring conflicts, hoping that they will resolve themselves. While all businesses have this tendency, the major issues presented in this chapter are inherent in family businesses and need to be addressed head-on because they will only get worse over time.

They Sleep with One Eye Open

Occasional squabbles among siblings are normal. In fact, I don't trust families that tell me their children always get along perfectly. But beyond the normal squabbles is a dark pathological realm of conflict where there are intense animosities and rivalries among the siblings. We're not talking about Wally's occasional irritations with the Beav; it's J.R. and Bobby Ewing.

I have a simple rule any time I encounter a family business with this kind of problem: keep the children out of the family's business, period.

THEY'RE NOT GOING TO WAKE UP ONE MORNING AND BE FRIENDS

The endurance capacity of siblings who are at war with one another is truly amazing. They will find ways to continue their fighting indefinitely, unless and until the underlying issues driving the conflict are resolved.

The problem is not curable by the parents. Unfortunately, when kids hate one another this much, parents are incapable of solving the problem. Remember, the parents created the family system that allowed these animosities and rivalries to flourish. If they helped create the mess, why should they be able to resolve it?

The parents won't live forever. Just look at what happened to Yugoslavia after Tito died. It took a few years, but no one was there to keep a lid on things and old animosities finally kicked in. Since parents don't live forever either, are there parallels in family businesses?

If the parents insist upon trying to ignore the problem, about the best they can hope to do is to keep a lid on it. This ignores the unfortunate reality that they're not always going to be around. When they do die, become incapacitated, or withdraw from the business—look out! Unrestricted warfare will erupt.

The family needs a doctor, not a referee or peacekeeper. The only chance of getting at the root cause of the problem is to stop ignoring it and bring in professional intervention. The family—immediate or extended—can't solve it.

The family needs to bring in someone who is specifically trained to identify, confront, and resolve problems arising within family systems. This means using a psychiatrist, a psychologist, or a good consultant—not a CPA or other general business advisor. Remember, this is not a business issue per se. Siblings will often yell and scream that they're fighting over purely business issues involving one another's incompetency or unfairness—but what they're really doing is using the business as an excuse to fight.

THE BUSINESS MUST NOT BE USED AS A CRUTCH

The family must always put the best interests of the business first if the business is to succeed. This means that the family cannot use it to try to resolve sibling conflict.

A placating tool. It's common to find parents who have been using the family business as a means of buying the children's peace. "Maybe our kids will get along if we give them jobs with big enough titles and pay them lavish salaries," parents think. Unfortunately, rather than rewarding their kids for good behavior, these parents are giving them a reward for not acting up. These kids are actually quite brilliant because they've figured out a way to extort their parents covertly.

Unfortunately, this practice wastes the business's resources.

A deep war chest. If the kids have been fighting all their lives, there's no reason to believe they won't use the business as a new arena. Not only is the change in venue exciting, it carries the additional benefit of access to the company's money to fund their warfare.

The family business enables these siblings to continue their fight along previously unavailable dimensions. Rather than fight conventionally for their parents and the world to see, they can now take the fight underground, using guerrilla warfare. Just think of all the possible intrigues people can engineer within a business. The permutations are mind-boggling.

Because there are numerous interdependencies within any business organization, siblings can successfully undermine one another without the other person (or the parents) knowing. In one company, the brother in charge of production made sure that delays occurred when he filled orders for his salesman brother's important clients. The delays always looked legitimate but occurred only with his brother and not with any other sales rep. In another company, the sister in charge of accounting would lose her brother's expense receipts, but only when his credit card was maxed out and he needed reimbursement.

THE EFFECT(S) OF THIS BEHAVIOR PATTERN

Such siblings will continue to re-create their conflicts and rivalries as they enter the business. The best interests of the business will take second priority to settling old scores.

"Hell No, We Won't Go"

Human mortality makes business succession inevitable. But unlike in large corporations, family-business succession involves many personal issues.

It's better for families to acknowledge the inevitable and address succession issues early rather than waiting for someone's imminent death or disability to create emotional distractions. It should be done while there's still the possibility of identifying and training successors.

SUCCESSION CREATES CHANGE

In a nutshell, business succession means that the current owners are going to be stepping aside and successors are going to move up and replace them. But we're talking about family businesses, which means that there are going to be other issues involved, mostly stemming from the interplay between the business and family systems.

Roles reverse (in the business system). In business, succession means that the parents depart and their children step into control. Within the business system, the children take on the dominant or "parent" role, while their parents assume passive/subservient or "child" roles.

Roles stay the same (in the family system). Succession does not alter the roles or orientation of people within the family system. The parents will forever be the parents and will retain their role as the head of the family system, and the kids will always be the kids (regardless of the fact that they're now running the business).

WHY DO PROBLEMS ARISE?

Succession alters the roles only within the business system, while the roles in the family system remain unchanged. Many families fail to understand this distinction, and the owners view stepping aside in the business as synonymous with relinquishing their role as head of the family.

The inability to distinguish business succession roles from

family roles creates two types of obstacles to planning for succession.

The parents are fearful . . . It's easy for parents to view succession planning as only the first phase in a series of events that will also place them in a subordinate or dependent role in the family system. They're aware that they are aging, and they know that aging often brings with it a series of issues involving health, capabilities, and so on.

Many owners fight to stay in control of the business, believing that that's the only way they can deny their own mortality. And who can blame them? Running the business may be a critical part of how they define themselves. Take that away, and they have no purpose.

. . . and so are their kids. Children sometimes wonder whether they are up to the challenge, because their skills must be equal to those of their parents. Have they been properly prepared, or have their growth and development been hampered?

If sufficiently dysfunctional, the children may view taking control of the business as betraying their parents' love. After all, their role is to be the children—anywhere, anyplace, any time. How can they love their parents and replace them at the same time?

Remember, keep the systems separated. Members of family businesses have two roles: as a member of the family and as a member of the business. Changing one's roles in one of these systems does not automatically mean changing roles in the other. With succession, the parties must learn how to interact with the children being the head of the business system while the parents are the titular heads of the family.

THE EFFECT(S) OF THIS BEHAVIOR PATTERN

The inability to differentiate between family and business roles may delay succession until it is forced upon the business and conducted in a crisis manner, possibly placing the business in danger.

"Who Invited Them?"

At a minimum, marriage brings a new member into the family system. It might also bring a new participant into the family business. The impact of these people is difficult to predict, so the family needs to draw boundaries regarding participation of spouses *before* their kids start getting married and stick to them afterward. In addition, the arrival of a new family member can innocently create tensions within the family.

A FAMILY MEMBER'S MARRIAGE DISRUPTS THINGS

The entry of a spouse into the family can cause disruption for a number of reasons. The family system must adjust to this new person; this usually involves no more than an awareness that somehow things are going to be a little different. But the extent that the business system should change depends on the family's wishes and the enforcement of good business practices.

A new spouse is a new partner. There is a correlation between the type of partner the new spouse becomes—silent, active, or agitator—and his or her potential for creating conflict.

At a minimum, the new spouse will become a silent or passive business partner, even if he or she has nothing to do with the family business. Do you think you won't talk about what happens at your family business? Can you possibly expect your spouse never to express an opinion about it? Not if the marriage is healthy. The new partner will have a de facto informal influence.

In other cases, the new spouse will insist on being an active copartner in the family's business. This may create tension with other family members, who have no problem with the entry of the spouse into the family system yet resent this person being forced onto them within the business system.

Finally, the new spouse may play the role of an interloper or agitator, which often occurs when an owner remarries and the new spouse wants the children from the prior marriage removed from the business system (i.e., resents their presence in the business or cuts the children out of possible inheritance). I know of one business where the new wife gave her husband an ultimatum: he'd have to fire his two sons, or she'd divorce him. She was jealous that these sons were a constant reminder of his ex-wife. Since the company was in a community property state, a divorce would have forced a liquidation of the family's business. Dad fired his sons, even though they were two of the company's best performers.

A threat to the status quo—"for better or for worse." New spouses do not automatically accept the values of the extended family they marry into. Why should they? After all, they were raised in their own family and bring those values with them.

In addition, a new spouse diverts the attention of his or her spouse away from both the family and the business. Other family members in the business may resent the distraction and believe they're having to carry extra work because this person is suddenly preoccupied.

I didn't marry my spouse; I got stuck with the whole family.
Will the new spouse resent the daily contact you have with
your family? While this is a natural consequence of being in the
family business, the new spouse may not have similar reasons
to stay in touch with his or her family and won't. But day in
and day out, all they'll hear about is your family, and they'll
probably pressure you to spend less time with them.

WHOM DO YOU SIDE WITH IF CONFLICT ARISES (AND NOT SUFFER CONSEQUENCES)?

There's no guarantee that in-laws and other family members
will get along with one another, and these conflicts in the
family system present special challenges for members of the
business system who try to maintain harmonious working
relations.

Family members who otherwise work well together are put
into a dilemma. Backing up their spouse's conflict with other
family members will disrupt the business even though it
pleases the spouse, while any cooperation or collaboration
with those in the business will be viewed as disloyalty by their
spouse. They're damned if they do and damned if they don't.

Fights among in-laws must not be allowed to affect the business. The family must commit itself to putting the best interests of the business first and must present a unified front
whenever this type of conflict occurs. It cannot ignore the
problem.

THE EFFECT(S) OF THIS BEHAVIOR PATTERN

Problems will arise if the family pretends that a marriage
changes nothing. Marriage creates changes in the family system, and failing to adjust to them will produce conflicts. The

business system does not automatically require adjustments because of marriage, and making adjustments without good business rationale will create problems.

The "Maybe It Will Go Away If We Ignore It" Syndrome

Failing to address problems that will inevitably emerge with increasing intensity and destructive potential.

Manifestation	Description	Effect(s)
They sleep with one eye open	Sibling conflict far beyond the "usual" squabbles.	The best interests of the business take second priority to fighting with one another.
"Hell no, we won't go"	Fear that succession is the first step in a process culminating with incapacity or death of the parents.	Succession is delayed until it is forced on the business, undermining its effectiveness.
"Who invited them?"	No adjustments are made to the family system or incorrect ones are made to the business system when someone marries into the family.	Conflict arises if the family system does not adjust for the new entrant or if the business system is forced to adjust without a good business rationale.

10

·········

"Tell Me About Your Childhood"

"Distance" means that people are removed from the direct pressures of their family system. In other words, they're free to do or be what they want; no one from the family is present to act as a controlling influence. Distance is achieved to a small extent when kids go off to summer camp or, more important, when they go off to college. The longer the time period and the less communication they have with their family, the greater the distance achieved.

So why is distance so important? Because it's the only way that people can discover themselves. Distance enables people to learn what their likes and dislikes are; what their strengths and weaknesses are. Perhaps most important, distance enables people to receive realistic feedback about themselves through their interactions with others. None of this is possible while a person is still under the strong influence of his or her family system.

Distance enables people to compare their "genetic predisposition"—their innate strengths, weaknesses, skills, abilities—against the career role that has been assigned to them by their family system. If people discover that they were really meant to do or be something else, distance gives them a chance to learn how to adapt and become what they were meant to be. This does not happen when they lack distance.

"I'm Still Waiting for That Pony"

Disappointments occur in any family as the children grow up, and the family system's continued pressure on them is a continual reminder of these events. Some wounds will never heal regardless of how much time elapses, while others may heal, provided that sufficient distance is achieved and maintained.

WHAT WAS THAT ALL ABOUT?

Conflicts among family members who work in the family business may erupt in unpredictable ways and at unpredictable times. Two family members will have a brief interaction on an innocuous subject, and suddenly—wham! It's all-out war.

The critical thing to recognize is that the conflict has absolutely nothing to do with the topic being discussed, even though that's what seems to be the cause. What's really happening is that the interaction between family members has triggered certain memories and/or emotions buried deep in one person's subconscious, and those emotions are what they're reacting to. Unfortunately, all the instigator felt were the painful emotions flaring up, and he or she reacted (or overreacted) accordingly.

How often does this happen in family businesses? Probably a lot more than most people realize. Anytime there's a pattern of people snapping at one another for no apparent reason, it's a good bet that this syndrome is present.

WHAT YOU SEE IS NOT WHAT YOU GET

What makes people snap at each other for no apparent reason? There are numerous possibilities, but there are usually two major causes.

The "piling-on" effect. In football, a penalty is called if a team piles onto someone carrying the ball. There's something inherently dangerous about eight or more 300-plus-pound guys jumping on top of one person—people inevitably get hurt.

Growing up in a family involves a series of disappointments. That's normal. In football, being tackled by one or two people doesn't usually cause injuries; the tackled person can get up, walk away, and shake it off. It's when too many people pile on in rapid succession that the weight becomes unbearable and people get hurt. In a family setting, people get hurt when they encounter a series of disappointments or painful situations without having time to recover. The hurt person will eventually explode.

This brings us back to the importance of distance. If a hurt person is working in the family business, the odds are that he or she never had time to get proper distance and let time heal his or her wounds. Continuing to work in the business only prevents the wounds from healing.

The straw that broke the camel's back. The instigator may be reacting to other family members' continual behavior patterns. These may involve something small, something inconsequential, that if it happened only once would not provoke such a strong reaction. But the recurrence of this dynamic over and over eventually causes the hurt family member to explode.

IT ONLY SEEMS INAPPROPRIATE

It's important to remember that things may seem nonsensical if they're viewed too literally. The fact that the instigator exploded at someone else makes absolutely no sense if you look only at the incident in question. What's needed is to step back and place it in a larger context.

The problem may be the result of history. Here the conflict is not a single isolated incident; it's a culmination of events. It's the totality of these incidents, undiminished by time, that creates the flare-ups.

The problem may be that person. The instigator exploded at another family member. In most cases, he or she would never have behaved that way had it been someone else, especially a non–family member. It's the fact that that person is a family member coupled with the fact that the person committed some perceived transgression in the past.

The problem must be probed more deeply. Anytime family members find themselves exploding at one another unexpectedly, they need to learn new behaviors. They need to learn to probe, to step back and look beyond what's happening whenever strong conflicts arise. They need to ask themselves, "What am I *really* angry about?" Realizing that they're overreacting in a manner that is inconsistent with the present situation will help them learn to deal with current interactions rather than chase past ghosts.

THE BUSINESS IS DISRUPTED

Such a pattern is disruptive to the family business because it hampers the ability of family members to interact effectively—and, ultimately, profitably—with one another.

People are baffled. Anytime a family member explodes in anger for no apparent reason, people get confused. The instigator may declare why he or she is angry, but to others it won't make sense. Since it's unlikely that the person who exploded knows why he or she really did so, it's not fair to expect others to guess the cause.

And if other family members are baffled, just imagine the impact on nonfamily employees. They can't possibly know all of the family's history, all the conflicts, the "dirt." They see only what's in front of them, and it won't make sense because the flare-up was totally out of proportion to the cause. But they'll be affected nonetheless.

People start to walk on eggs. If the flare-ups are sufficiently nasty, everyone—family and employees alike—may be fearful of recurrences. Sadly, what they do to try to prevent those recurrences may not be good for the business.

Since family members get angry at one another for no apparent reason, the most logical step is for people to avoid addressing "tough" issues. The irony is that the conflicts generally have absolutely nothing to do with these tough issues, and addressing them won't necessarily cause conflict. It's essential to the business that tough issues be addressed head-on, but an environment where people are walking on eggs is not conducive to resolving them.

In such situations people compensate to try to prevent conflicts, but what they do doesn't address the root problem. People take actions to solve problems that don't exist while creating and/or avoiding other problems for the business. For example, I was in one meeting where the family members thought they were fighting about the purchase of machinery. They weren't, but the fight was intense and they ended up making a poor business decision just to end the fight. Unfortunately, fearing a repeat of the earlier argument, they then refused to discuss future equipment purchases with one another, even though what they were really fighting about had nothing to do with purchasing machinery.

THE EFFECT(S) OF THIS BEHAVIOR PATTERN

In addition to a strained working environment, the effect of inexplicable conflicts is that people will take inappropriate actions to try to prevent recurrences. Difficult issues may not be addressed, or people will hesitate to interact with one another and communicate, solve problems, or share information.

"My Kids Must Be Great Because I'm Their Parent"

When we think of child abuse, we're filled with repugnant images of inexcusable outrages inflicted upon innocent children. Unfortunately, there's another form of child abuse, one that seems to go unrecognized, if not actually sanctioned or glorified by society. I'm talking about situations where parents view their children's overachievements as their own. Since they believe that their children are extensions of themselves, these parents place unrealistically high expectations upon their children. Any achievements or accomplishments of the children are then considered to be a direct reflection of the parents' own greatness.

BUT THEY'RE ONLY CHILDREN

They seem to be everywhere, children who are pushed by their parents into performing unnatural feats: seven-year-olds who are expected to fly an airplane cross-country, six-year-olds who are expected to put on adult makeup and perform in "beauty" contests. Whatever happened to simply encouraging kids to play in the neighborhood soccer league?

120

Unattainable expectations. The children of these parents have totally unattainable expectations placed upon them. Anything less than absolute perfection or superhuman accomplishment is not acceptable. But do these children have the mental capacity to comprehend what they're expected to do? Have their bodies developed sufficiently to allow them to perform these tasks? No—they are not allowed to be just average kids.

Any mistake is unforgivable. Since these children must be perfect, the slightest error is harshly punished or criticized. These errors unwittingly show that the parents themselves aren't perfect. The kids do not want to incur their parents' wrath, so they focus their attention on not making mistakes rather than on learning.

But the only way for someone to truly learn is to occasionally make mistakes. Mistakes allow people to depart from the known and well-traveled path, to take chances, to learn. Children whose primary emphasis is on avoiding mistakes to avoid punishment aren't free to take chances.

Instantaneously all-knowing. As they enter their family's business, the parents of these children expect them to automatically know everything there is about the business, even though it often took the parents several decades to build it (while learning in the process). There was plenty the parents didn't know, they probably learned via trial and error, and they surely made a lot of mistakes along the way. But this will not be tolerated of their children.

No escape. In a non-family-business situation, such children may have the opportunity to flee their family. It's that distance thing again. They can go work someplace else, move to another town, possibly join the Witness Protection Program. But there's no place to flee from these parents in a family business. What would have been an unfortunate childhood with the possibility to escape further damage becomes a never-ending cycle.

THEY NEVER HAD A CHILDHOOD

In a sense, these children never had a childhood. They were forced to be perfect little adults, to always excel. They were never allowed to be carefree and have fun like other kids. Instead, they grow into adulthood questioning their own abilities. Whatever their success, they somehow don't believe they're good enough.

I once counseled a successful executive in his mid-forties. He graduated with honors from one of the top MBA programs and had successfully completed every assignment given to him in his family's company. Yet deep down he felt like a failure because he never felt his parents accepted him unconditionally. It was only when he had accomplished some great feat that they acknowledged him. He would have traded all his money and his position atop his family's business for the feeling of being loved and accepted for what he was. Instead, he felt like a parolee on continual probation.

THE EFFECT(S) OF THIS BEHAVIOR PATTERN

The effect of these parental expectations on the children is to produce people entering the family's business who are plagued by nagging doubts about their abilities because they were never able to live up to their parents' expectations. In addition, they inevitably have feelings of resentment: at their parents for doing what they did, at the things that they were forced to do that other kids didn't have to. As a result, they may hate the family business and what they do within it.

"My Kid's the Greatest"

Though the title of this section sounds as though it's similar to the preceding one, the dynamics are totally different. Rather than view their children and the children's achievements as an extension of themselves (i.e., their kids' achievements are theirs), these parents are incapable of seeing any flaws whatsoever in their children. Instead, they blindly believe their kids are perfect.

YOUR LITTLE JOHNNY AIN'T SO PRECIOUS

Unfortunately, they teach their kids that they are precious, and if the kids never achieve sufficient distance to be provided with a reality check, there will be trouble.

Kids know only what their parents teach them. These parents continually tell their children how great they are. Anything their children do is met with lavish and unrestricted praise. Their kids are always the center of attention and can do no wrong.

Over time, the kids actually begin to believe these untruths. And why not? It feels great to believe them.

Reality may be entirely different. Unfortunately, there's no possibility of gaining objectivity on one's performance when parents heap unreserved praise onto a child. Everything suggests that there's nothing to improve.

This provides the children with a seemingly no-lose situation. They can continue to do whatever they have done in the past, or they will do whatever they want.

THIS KID DOES NOT "KNOW THYSELF"

Sadly, these children will grow into adults with a totally distorted self-image.

They believe they're better than they really are. These children have always been the center of attention and have heard that everything they do is wonderful. They grow up with a completely overinflated ego, which is my polite way of saying that they're spoiled little brats in need of a serious attitude adjustment.

They are clueless about their flaws or weaknesses. Raising children in this manner condemns them to be unable to develop further. Their assumption is that there's nothing to improve. How could there be? They've never been told there is. The combination of being clueless and spoiled means they will refuse to see any signs of their possible flaws.

They avoid "distance" at all costs. If these kids get sufficient distance from their family, they'll surely begin to receive negative feedback about themselves. Their parents will tell them that it simply isn't true—that they are perfect—and it's easy to believe what their parents are telling them because it feels better.

If they are subjected to enough negative feedback, they will often reduce the distance and come back under the direct control of their family. They're not used to hearing anything unpleasant about themselves, so even the slightest negative feedback has a traumatic effect. They want to protect their ego at all costs and will therefore return to the safety of their family system.

They're a Danger to Themselves, Others, and the Family Business. These people have a definite impact on the family business, and it's generally not positive.

They're sheer hell to work for (with). Because they are not as competent as they believe, they're bound to make mistakes. But since they think they're flawless, problems will *never* be their fault. They will always be someone else's fault, and they'll be sure to blame others. They'll take credit for everything that goes right and blame others for all setbacks. Working for their family's business gives them the power to do this.

These spoiled kids grow up to be particularly effective at destroying morale. At best, they'll be very demanding and unappreciative of the contributions other people make, while expecting them to be subservient. At worst, they'll be abusive towards others in the business.

They don't know what they don't know. Having never received critical feedback, these people often assume that whatever they do is right—and that it will be successful. Having never been told the truth, they easily overestimate their own abilities and underestimate new competitive threats in the marketplace. I know of a son who refused to affiliate his family's hardware store with a national chain: "We don't need it." A few years later, he refused a chance to invest in a large do-it-yourself home improvement franchise: "People want to buy from our family." Today, the family business doesn't exist, and the do-it-yourself franchise is prospering.

The reality is that they don't know everything, but there's nothing to bring them down to reality.

THE EFFECT(S) OF THIS BEHAVIOR PATTERN

The effect of raising a child in this manner is to produce someone who is completely out of touch with their abilities. Rather than raising a competent new member of the family business, the family produces a monster who is a spoiled child in the

125

body of an adult. If the child eventually takes over the business, experience has proven over and over again that he or she will probably ruin it.

The "Tell Me About Your Childhood" Syndrome

Children enter the family business before experiencing sufficient "distance" to resolve critical issues from their childhood.

Manifestation	Description	Effect(s)
"I'm still waiting for that pony"	Unresolved disagreements and disappointments continue on into the business.	Conflicts erupt in unforeseen ways and at unexpected times. People take inappropriate action to prevent recurrences.
"My kid must be great because I'm their parent"	Parents view children's achievements (i.e., overachievements) as their own.	Children plagued by self-doubt; resentment at parents and the family's business.
"My kid's the greatest"	Parents are oblivious to flaws in or problems with their children.	Children have a distorted self-image: an inflated sense of self-worth and self-assessment; clueless about their deficiencies. Possibly abusive toward others.

PART III

Succession

A Battleground unto Itself

Do not go gentle into that good night,
Old age should burn and rave at close of day;
Rage, rage against the dying of the light.

Though wise men at their end know dark is right,
Because their words had forked no lightning they
Do not go gentle into that good night.

Good men, the last wave by, crying how bright
Their frail deeds might have danced in a green bay,
Rage, rage against the dying of the light.

Wild men who caught and sang the sun in flight,
And learn, too late, they grieved it on its way,
Do not go gentle into that good night.

Grave men, near death, who see with blinding sight
Blind eyes could blaze like meteors and be gay,
Rage, rage against the dying of the light.

> And you, my father, there on the sad height,
> Curse, bless, me now with your fierce tears, I pray.
> Do not go gentle into that good night.
> Rage, rage against the dying of the light.

The preceding is:

1. A classic Dylan Thomas poem
2. Eerily familiar
3. The AARP mission statement

This is actually a trick question because the correct answer is "All of the above." Succession in family businesses is never about succession. If it were, it would be a manageable process. But it's not. It never is. And there the trouble begins, which is why I condemn most outside advisors who try to coach families through succession planning—they never understand this simple reality.

The group of outside advisors that family businesses almost always rely upon to help them with succession planning is accountants. True to their accountant ways, they see the world as a set of impersonal numbers on a balance sheet, thinking the answers must lie in somehow getting things to add up just right.

You must ensure that your business follows the information presented in the next four chapters; otherwise your succession is doomed to fail because it's viewed only from the perspective of your accountant's green eyeshades.

> Do not go gentle into that bad advice.
> Rage, rage against the dying of their insight.

11

···········

Certain Problems Are
Inherent to Succession

No matter how healthy the family system or how well run the family business, succession is one of those things that creates problems for almost everyone involved.

It's Not a Clash Between the Forces of Good and Evil; It's Merely Change Versus Constancy

The process of succession puts two opposing states in conflict with each other: change and constancy. As you will see, change provokes strong feelings in most people.

THERE ARE EXPECTATIONS OF CHANGE ARISING FROM SUCCESSION

What's a more profound change for a business than to have one set of owners step aside for another? Naturally, people are going to assume that a lot of changes are going to occur.

One state is comfortable (even though it's potentially danger- ous) . . . Constancy is comfortable for people and organizations, and the people in the family business have a built-in bias to try to keep things in this state. People know what is expected of them and what to expect from others, how to do things and how things are done. There's an order and predictability that make people feel safe.

But should they? Any business operates in a constantly changing environment, and the status quo mentality that exists when the organization is in constancy can represent a threat to its continuing existence.

... while the other state isn't (even though it's usually the safest). Change, on the other hand, produces uncertainty, fear, and discomfort. People hate it.

Change requires that people adapt to new sets of circumstances, but what these new circumstances will be is not known. Added to this is the personal uncertainty of not knowing whether they will be able to make the required transition. And there's more: How does anyone know whether this is the right change to make? However painful, change is usually necessary to keep the business in touch with its marketplace.

Why all this conflict with succession? The process of undergoing succession means that change is probable, and that isn't always pleasant. A new group of owners and/or leaders is coming into the business, bringing with them their own set of values, beliefs, and ambitions. If people in the business want to be successful, they will have to adapt to these new styles. If the style and practices of the successors are similar to those of their predecessors, the amount of change required within the organization will be minimal. But if the new styles and practices are significantly different, the successors will be demanding significant change. Will the employees be able to adapt?

It's important for successors to understand that their very

presence within the business will engender fear. Fear results in resistance, so people will present obstacles to change. Successors have to be ready to address these obstacles.

REASONS PEOPLE AVOID SUCCESSION PLANNING

Business owners do their best to avoid doing succession planning for a number of reasons, often stemming from personal or psychological resistance. It's important to remember that resistance is not limited to family businesses; it also runs rampant through non-family-owned *Fortune* 500 companies.

Succession planning raises unpleasant family issues. Many families place a premium on family harmony and are aware that in order to conduct succession planning they will have to deal with a number of potentially explosive issues. Among these issues are: identifying the successor(s) and, more important, who is *not* going to be the successor; determining who gets how much and what type of ownership; and deciding how they will announce these unpleasant decisions to others.

Because they expect pain and conflict, owners often prefer to defer all succession issues indefinitely rather than confront (and possibly resolve) them.

Succession forces people to confront their mortality. While death is inevitable, people don't like to be reminded of it. The process of conducting succession planning forces business owners to explicitly acknowledge that they are not going to live forever. What's worse, there are a series of issues that must be addressed and actions taken that continually reenforce this reality. These people will have to determine the value of their estate and probably be forced to write or rewrite their will. For most people, that brings death too close for comfort.

People are too busy doing day-to-day tasks. Who has time to do all this planning crap? Business owners, especially if they're entrepreneurs, prefer to spend their time doing hands-on tasks. Succession planning is an altogether different process. It requires them to step back and do some reflective thinking—the very antithesis of performing hands-on tasks.

Some business owners take this to an extreme: they'll *make* themselves far too busy to have the time to perform succession-planning activities.

The owner fears suffering a loss of control. Not surprisingly, most family-business owners have a strong need for control. But properly performing succession planning requires them to give up a lot of it. They'll have to depend on other people for advice as well as for implementing succession plans. To a business owner, being dependent on other people is uncomfortable, if not unbearable.

Also, people with a strong need to control tend to restrict the dissemination of information. But succession planning cannot be done properly if the owner does not share significant information with others, and that's something many owners simply do not want to do. What they fail to realize is that the only way for succession plans to make sense to people in the organization is if those people understand the reasoning behind the succession planning.

The owner fears that a succession plan will reduce options. Business owners like to keep as many options open as possible. Their nature is to generate a lot of ideas and options. If they're entrepreneurs, they've been rewarded for generating and capitalizing on possibilities no one else saw.

These owners will argue that succession planning cannot be done because future uncertainty makes it impossible for them to determine which options to select and implement. Technically they're correct, because a succession plan requires that a business focus its energies on a discrete number of options. But if the plan is created properly, the options selected are not so narrowly focused as to be overly restrictive. Also, they're not forever carved in stone.

The process of focusing on discrete options is so foreign to the way many owners operate their business that they simply can't do it.

They don't know how to plan. Sometimes that's all there is to it. A danger with consultants (myself excluded, of course) is that they sometimes want to project their own biases into a situation, looking for dark psychological or organizational underpinnings to explain why succession planning is avoided. Instead, the simple reason that owners have not performed succession planning is often that they don't know how.

Succession planning is not an innate skill. It requires professionals with a set of acquired skills and specialized knowledge. Yet many business owners do not like to admit that they do not know how to perform succession planning because admitting this makes them feel inept. If this is you, just remember: your business advisors and consultants—if they're worth having—learned how to do what they do only after years of education and experience. It's not something they were born knowing.

It's All in the Timing

Many of the problems and conflicts associated with succession are largely a result of timing issues—a function of when the succession will take place. But don't get the notion that succession is problem-free if you perform it at the "correct" time.

133

Like so many other things with family businesses, if succession occurs at the "correct" time one set of issues and conflicts arises, while if it doesn't occur at the "correct" time there's an entirely different set.

SUCCESSION SHOULD BE TIMED TO MATCH THE SUCCESSORS' ABILITIES

Assuming that intergenerational succession within the family will occur, the fundamental principle regarding when it should occur is as follows: it should be timed to occur when the successors are entering their years of maximum ability—their prime. The reason for this is that the business needs the most qualified leaders it can get and the successors will be most capable to take over the business when their abilities are at their strongest.

How do you measure ability? Unfortunately, measuring the abilities of owners and would-be successors—how capable they are to run the family's business—is not a precise science. How do you know what the most important abilities are? What measurements can you use to accurately compare different peoples' abilities? Unless there are blatant differences between people, this often boils down to a judgment call.

One of the biggest difficulties is knowing when the would-be successors' abilities are beginning to match those of the people currently in charge of the business. If succession should be timed to correspond with the successors' abilities, shouldn't it be conducted when the successors' abilities match those of the people in power? Yes, assuming that the people in power are members of an older generation (i.e., Mom and Dad) and that their abilities are going to be gradually diminishing. Again, how do you measure this?

What usually happens with family businesses is that the would-be successors are well into middle age while the current leaders are still firmly in control (with no desire to leave). This can create tremendous frustration for the would-be successors, who feel stifled.

What do you do with the people in power? Just because the abilities of the would-be successors are beginning to match those of the people currently in power, it does not mean that the people who are in power have lost any of their value. If they're still valuable, why should they step aside? Therein lies the problem.

To conform to the key principle of this section, the current owners and leaders must often step aside and take early retirement in order to make room for the successors in waiting. But the notion of sitting in a retirement home and doing nothing is not particularly appealing to most people who run a business. Remember, these people are by no means "incapable"—their abilities are supposed to be closely matched with those of the people who are replacing them.

There has to be a continuing role for them. One of the keys to conducting succession well is finding alternative roles for the people currently in power. These alternative roles generally take one of two forms: remaining in the business and working on narrowly defined activities or projects while the successors take over running the business, or engaging in philanthropy or public service work. In either case, the role is going to have to be meaningful if the owners are to step aside willingly.

THE TIMING PROBLEM: ILLUSTRATED

The concept of timing succession to coincide with the successors' abilities, and the corresponding tasks, issues, and potential conflicts, is illustrated in Figure 6.

The first thing you'll notice about Figure 6 is that there are two identical curves. These curves reflect people's ability throughout their career. The curves represent life cycles, with people increasing in ability as they grow and mature, followed by a plateau when they are in their prime, followed by the eventual decline with the advancement of age.

The curve to the left is labeled "First generation." This corresponds to the current owners of the business. The curve to the right is labeled "Second generation" and in most cases represents the current owners' children.

The vertical axis of this diagram is "Ability." The higher up the vertical axis, the greater people's abilities. The horizontal axis, labeled "Career/Working Age" represents the number of years people work over the course of their life. The lower-left-hand corner represents when people begin working; moving across the page to the right corresponds to the passing of years until they eventually withdraw from their working years.

Finally, you'll notice that there are three separate milestones—grooming, succession, and conflict—which are shown by dotted vertical lines. Each of these represents a specific set of issues and problems, which are explained in detail below.

The best way for you to understand Figure 6 is for you to actively participate as I walk you through it. You can do this by taking out a pen and laying it vertically flat on the page, close to the left-hand side near the vertical axis labeled "Ability." (Remember, I'm asking you to lay your pen flat on the page— you don't want to draw or make marks on the diagram!)

FIGURE 6

Timing Succession to the Successors' Abilities

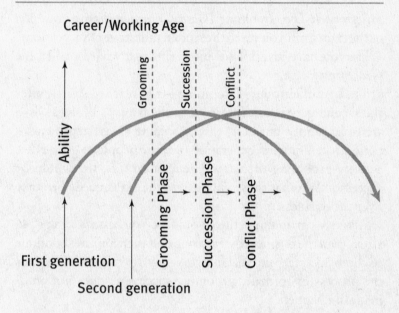

The parents start the business. As your pen lies on the page, you should see a little bit of the "First generation" curve to the left of it. Now slowly slide your pen to the right until you get to the first milestone: "Grooming." What do you see?

As you slide your pen to the right, the first generation is gaining in years and experience on the job and their curve is rising, meaning that their abilities are getting stronger. Then you'll notice that the second generation begins to enter the family's business. You should also notice that their absolute abilities are significantly less than the abilities of the first generation. This is one of those rare moments when the parents might actually be both older and wiser. Finally, you should notice that the curve for the second generation is rising much more steeply than that of the first generation.

Milestone 1: The Grooming Phase. Continue sliding your pen to the right until you reach the second milestone: "Succession." What you have just done is move through what is called the *Grooming Phase.*

The first milestone—Grooming—was reached shortly after the second generation entered into the family's business. In a well-run family business, the Grooming Phase represents a period when the first generation (i.e., the people in power) are actively grooming the second generation (i.e., the would-be successors) so that they will possess the skills needed to take over the business.

Actively grooming the would-be successors helps to strengthen the business by ensuring that their abilities continue to climb up a steep curve. Unfortunately, for numerous reasons the process of formally grooming successors does not automatically happen.

Milestone 2: The Succession Phase. Continue sliding your pen to the right until you reach the third and final milestone: "Conflict." This represents the *Succession Phase.*

During this phase, an interesting thing happens: the abilities of the second generation overtake and slightly surpass those of the first generation. Remember, measuring people's abilities is not a precise science, so there's no way to specify the exact date when succession should occur. The goal is for it to happen when the successors' abilities are entering their prime, and this is often the time when the abilities of both generations are roughly equal. There is no specific date when succession must occur, but it is best performed sometime within this phase.

Milestone 3: The Conflict Phase. Finally, continue moving your pen to the right. What do you see? You see that if succession has not occurred by the time the second generation's abilities have surpassed those of the first generation, the third phase—the *Conflict Phase*—is reached.

Conflict occurs because the second generation sees that the abilities of the first generation—those still in power—are diminishing while their own are strong and still increasing. Besides the personal frustration they feel, they also see that the business they will inherit is being weakened because of these lesser and diminishing skills of the people still in power.

Conflict between the generations will inevitably erupt, further undermining and weakening the business's viability. Ironically, this is not reflected in the curves as they are drawn in Figure 6 because the true effect varies according to the family. Once this conflict erupts, the curves will drop more steeply than they are drawn for both generations.

Some warnings about Figure 6. Remember, Figure 6 is meant to be illustrative. I had to make a few assumptions in order to do this.

First, the shape of the curves is arbitrary. It's possible that people's abilities increase less quickly, that they plateau longer, and that they don't diminish as rapidly.

Second, you'll notice that I drew identical curves, but there is no reason to believe that the second-generation curve will be identical to the first-generation curve. If you've read Part II of this book, you've already seen that sometimes the abilities of the second generation will never be equal to those of the first generation.

But it's also possible that the second generation will be much more talented than the first generation. If this happens, it will only intensify the problems I've described because the second generation will be ready to take over the business at a much earlier age, and since their potential abilities are that much better than their parents', there will be a much wider gap between the curves when the Conflict Phase is entered. The wider the gap, the greater the reason for conflict.

Warning Signs of a Difficult Succession Process

There are several warning signs that signal that a company's succession process is going to be difficult. Consultants and business advisors, as well as business owners, should be aware of these.

THE OWNER USES A "DOMINEERING" LEADERSHIP STYLE

We just can't get away from these people. It's probably because they seem to be everywhere and they're successful at creating problems (both for themselves and for their businesses). So what problems will they create for the succession process?

A weak management team and/or prospective successors. People need to learn certain skills if they are to survive working for a domineering owner. One of them is the ability to act weak. Remember, we're talking about a domineering owner— one with a strong need to control things and other people— and this is not necessarily an "abusive" person. People might not walk around in fear of this person yelling at them, but they do know not to assert themselves against him.

Although they might be otherwise talented, often the prospective successors and key managers have learned not to think for themselves, and they've learned not to take initiative.

Why? Because these actions preempt and challenge a dominant leader—precisely the sort of behavior that can get them into trouble.

Limitation of the successors' experience. Another problem with a domineering owner is that he tends to limit his subordinates' depth of experience. As a result, the prospective successors will have had a limited range of experience to apply when solving problems. They can't see the big picture.

A difficult working relationship for outside advisors. Even though they might have hired a consultant or other advisor, domineering owners feel a need to continually challenge these advisors' independence. But they're often clever, and they won't always challenge their advisors directly.

The usual practice is for these owners to present a series of obstacles or objections. While these may seem reasonable on the surface, what's really being objected to is the owner's inability to dominate the outside advisor. I once presented my findings to an owner who responded, "You didn't interview all my employees." When I returned, he then said, "You have insufficient data about my chief competitor." When I returned again, he said, "There is a pending development that only I am aware of," but he never did tell me what it was. Fortunately, my contract allowed me to bill him for this additional work.

Rather than responding to the objections presented (which in reality are red herrings), outside advisors need to quietly but forcefully assert themselves against these domineering owners (this is best done in private).

THERE IS A SENIOR MANAGEMENT GROUP WITH LONG TENURE

Long-tenured senior managers can make succession planning difficult in several ways.

They all think the same. People with long relationships and a history of common experiences tend to think alike. It's a self-reinforcing process, and any ideas that do not conform to their preconceived notions will be resisted or summarily dismissed.

Succession requires many changes from an organization and its people. A group with a rigid, uniform way of thinking may present a formidable obstacle to the successors' ability to implement change.

They're all the same age, and they're not young. A group of long-tenured senior managers suggests a lack of younger managers coming up within the company's ranks. Several of these managers might retire in rapid order, leaving the company without experienced managers.

They're resentful. Even though long-tenured managers tend to be loyal to the owner and the company, the reality is that even though they've been there a long time, they're not going to be taking over. Someone from the family is. To make matters worse, that person might be younger and not have worked there as long.

It's natural for them to feel a little resentful. Their long tenure didn't enable any of them to step into the role of successor.

THE COMPANY IS A FAMILY BUSINESS

The fact that a company is a family business is often a warning sign that the succession process is going to be difficult.

They're secretive. Family businesses tend to be exempt from the reporting and disclosure requirements of publicly traded companies (because in most cases they're not publicly traded). This means that they're used to operating with secrecy in many matters.

But to conduct succession properly, the owners are going to have to share a lot of information that they believe is sensitive: income, profitability, the value of their estate and assets, and so on. Advisors working with these companies are likely to encounter resistance when they try to obtain this information or when they try to share it with others in the business who have a need to know.

They're not used to outsiders. Family businesses often have a long tradition of not using outside advice, preferring instead to keep matters within the "family." The people who have been serving as advisors (e.g., accountants, attorneys, bankers) are often longtime family friends. In reality, they're members of an "extended family" rather than true outsiders such as the advisor now being called in. Winning the trust and confidence of these clients can be difficult.

12
·············

The Baggage Returns in Time for Succession

You didn't think we could discuss succession without having the family baggage emerge, did you? It's there, in full force.

The Sins of the Father . . .

Ever wonder why the owner seems so damn obstinate? Every family business should create and implement plans for a smooth succession, yet few owners will cooperate with this process. Succession planning without the owner's cooperation is an exercise in frustration.

FEARS THAT ARISE AS RETIREMENT APPROACHES

People often develop a number of fears as they approach their retirement. These will be fears they've never faced before because retirement presents a whole new set of issues. This is also a time when retirement is no longer some abstract notion—it's a distinct reality.

"The business is my nest egg." For a lot of family-business owners, the business is their major—if not sole—asset. Okay, they might also own their house, but that's not going to help provide for retirement. IRAs are a relatively recent phenomenon, so they probably haven't had a viable option for getting the benefits of a tax-deferred nest egg. Having the business as their retirement nest egg means that they are financially dependent on that business.

Remember, people approaching retirement don't have their entire career ahead of them. They don't have time to rebuild or recover their financial strength if a serious setback to the business occurs. This creates a dilemma for them: How can they know that the successors are up to running the business and won't destroy their asset? No, the safe option is for them to remain in control rather than hand their asset off to untried successors.

Why not just sell it, take the money and run? It's not that easy. The owner may be contractually prevented from doing so. Even if they can sell, will an outsider want to buy it? If their kids are the successors, can their kids afford to buy it? Where will they get the money? It's possible they can obtain a loan and buy the business, but a loan carries a burden of debt that might undermine the business's viability.

Some unpleasant things are happening to others around you. It's not a pretty sight: people nearing retirement often witness many of their longtime friends becoming disabled, dying, or moving into retirement homes. These are painful developments to watch and make business owners wonder whether similar experiences await them. Suddenly they feel very insecure.

Staying in control of their business now takes on a symbolic meaning. Owners can try to demonstrate their prowess by continuing to work, and they may actually prolong their prowess. Recent studies suggest that retirement—forced retirement, that is—may be a leading cause of death among people over the age of sixty-five.

My business is my life. Many people have worked so long and hard at their business that it has become an inseparable part of themselves. For years their business has been what has kept them going, and their identity is wrapped up in it. They *are* Smith Tool & Die, and they'll feel lost without it.

PERSONAL OBSTACLES TO BE OVERCOME

Succession presents a number of personal concerns that may cause people to resist it.

Diminished stature. A certain amount of power goes with being the owner and head of a company, and all of it will disappear when the owner steps aside. Does this person enjoy a certain standing in his community because he is the head of his company? Will this disappear when he steps aside?

Ironically, it's not always the business owner (i.e., the person in charge of the company) who's the problem. In some situations the business owner's spouse derives a lot of his or her identity through the spouse's business role, and he or she fears that succession will eliminate this source of stature. These spouses will resist retirement as well.

A potential solution for diminished stature? The solution often resides within people's own psyche. Business owners need to understand that their accomplishments, achievements, and successes can't be taken away from them. These stand on their own, regardless of whether they continue in their role as head of a business.

One way to help overcome this obstacle is to create a new role for the person stepping aside. This role is often what might be called "elder statesman." It's critical to remember that the person stepping aside still has significant knowledge, insight, and personal contacts and represents a tremendous value to the business. Successors are well advised to find a way to utilize this expertise.

"I haven't . . ." People seldom accomplish all of the goals they set for themselves in life, and these unrealized goals may become a sensitive issue as succession nears. It doesn't matter how much has been achieved; owners may become obsessed with the things they haven't accomplished and insist on retaining control of their business in order to pursue these unaccomplished objectives.

A solution to "I haven't . . ."? Again, a solution to this obstacle is often to create a role for the former owner. In this case, the role is often that of consultant to the business.

If the successors agree that the predecessor's unfulfilled objectives are important for the business, they should continue to employ the predecessor to pursue special projects that focus on these unfulfilled objectives. In fact, many business owners find that only once they've stepped aside are they able to successfully complete these unfulfilled objectives, because as consultants they are shielded from the day-to-day distractions of running the business that often kept them from getting the task accomplished.

Loss of identity. Many people derive their identity from their work. Succession removes owners from their business role, thereby threatening their identity.

This is different from the "My Business Is My Life" phenomenon described earlier. There, I described people who identify themselves with their company so closely that they begin to think they are the company. Here, I'm talking about an identity related to one's occupation or vocation. For example, a business owner may have studied engineering and spent his or her early years as an engineer. Even though he or she is the head of a company, at heart he or she identifies with engineers.

A solution to loss of identity? This is a hard obstacle to overcome because the solution often lies in finding a new venue that enables these people to practice their "vocation." Since the vocation is often very technical, there's no room for them to practice it in the business because they would be taking a role clearly subservient to the successors', and the presence of a former owner in such a role creates its own set of problems for the business. Instead, these alternate venues might include teaching, active involvement in professional organizations or associations, and possibly participation in a philanthropic organization.

Often, only when they step aside do owners get to engage in their true vocation. As heads of businesses, they had to perform leadership functions, which meant they didn't have time to engage in technical work.

. . . Will Be Visited upon His Children . . .

Even if the owner agrees it's time to step down, certain issues will face the children who are taking over the business.

WHEN TO ANNOUNCE THAT ONE OF YOUR CHILDREN WILL REPLACE YOU

Business owners often struggle with the thorny issue of when to identify and select which of their children will take over the business. They believe—often correctly—that by doing so they will show preference or favoritism toward one of the children, thereby creating significant conflict within the family. They figure they can maintain family harmony by delaying the inevitable. Unfortunately, things don't work that way.

There are two realities that cannot be escaped. First, the owner of the business is eventually going to die, become disabled, retire, or otherwise be replaced. Second, because the business needs a leader, someone will have to step in and replace the owner. Therefore, it's in the family's best interest to identify and announce the child who will be taking over the business *as early as possible*. In addition, the selection of any successor must be based upon rational criteria that put the best interests of the business ahead of the feelings of any family members.

There are three main advantages to doing this.

It provides time to resolve conflicts before the actual succession. So the parents' worst fears do come true and there's significant family conflict. By making the announcement well in advance of the actual succession, the parents are still firmly in control of their business and can impose the measures needed to restore harmony. The children who feel that they were wrongly passed over will have ample opportunity to express their views (and you can bet they will!). The parents will have ample time to articulate their reasons for making their decision to both family members and employees. Finally, while the parents are still in control, they'll have time and energy to help create other options for the children who were passed over and to enforce their decision if need be.

Remember that this advantage assumes that the owner is healthy enough to do this. This is not always the case, so the family may need to bring in outside advisors to help.

The people who were passed over still have time to pursue other options. Several of the kids have invested a lot of time and energy in their family's business, believing that they would assume leadership. When they learn that they're not going to be the successor, they're going to be pissed—really pissed. This anger is amplified in direct proportion to the amount of time and energy they have invested in the business. An early announcement of who the successor will be reduces—if not eliminates—the amount of time the nonsuccessors will waste in false hope.

Perhaps the most important benefit of an early announcement is that it lets everyone know where they stand. However painful it may seem at the time, the knowledge that they are not going to take control of their family's business is actually a gift because they are now free to explore other career options and, most important, to do so at a time when they are (hopefully) still young enough to go in other career directions.

An unfortunate but common scenario occurs when middle-aged children, after having spent their entire career working for their family's business, learn that they will be passed over for leadership. Even the post office treats its employees more humanely (and you know what postal employees do when they get mad). Nonsuccessors usually find that the experience and skills gained from working in the family business are too limited to enable them to pursue a meaningful career path elsewhere. They are now captives of their family's business. For example, I know of a son who left college in his third year to take over the operations of the family's printing company. For twenty-plus years he focused on mastering every technical detail of the family business, then learned that his cousin would instead be put in charge. While he knew everything about the family company, he found that how his family operated its business was far different from how others in the industry did. What he'd learned couldn't be transferred elsewhere.

The process resolves uncertainty within the organization. People within an organization tend to work better when they know what is happening, and a family business is no exception. It's amazing how few leaders of organizations understand this concept. In fact, there are times when hearing even bad news— however unpleasant—has a better effect on employee morale than being kept wondering.

Not knowing who the owner's successor will be creates uncertainty, which reduces employees' productivity. Removing uncertainty by telling people who the successor will be frees them to focus their energy and attention on performing their jobs.

OBSTACLES YOUR CHILDREN WILL FACE WHEN THEY TAKE YOUR PLACE

Children who take over from their parents face several obstacles that aren't present in traditional business situations.

Other people are envious or suspicious of them. Successors-to-be often find that some people are uncomfortable interacting with them. They have to be on guard not to let these interactions taint their feelings toward these employees.

First, there's the fear factor. Employees are often fearful of an up-and-coming successor because they realize that this person will someday be their boss, yet they don't know how this successor will treat them once they take over. As a result of these fears, they often find themselves a little on guard in their interactions.

Then there's the envy factor. It's hard to blame employees who feel a little resentful toward the successor-to-be, viewing him or her as a privileged child who gained the position through birthright rather than merit.

"Okay, kid, prove yourself." Resentment often causes people to deny any talents or abilities the successor might in fact possess.

Since the only reason successors got their position is because they were born to it, they often need to prove themselves and overcome the stigma of "birthright." They do this by demonstrating their abilities, but the birthright stigma means they will have to perform at a higher level than any successor coming from the outside.

They were promoted too quickly. Many parents feel compelled to promote their children as rapidly as possible. While they think they're doing them a favor, it's actually a disservice because the kids are denied two types of learning. First, fully understanding their family's business and being able to see the big picture requires them to spend some time at various positions throughout the business. Second, developing strong leadership skills requires years of practice.

If the kids haven't had a chance to fully learn from each position before moving up, the result is successors who appear to have better-developed skills than they actually possess.

"That's not how your dad did it." One of the first things successors find is that every action they take is compared against

the benchmark of what their predecessor would have done. These continual comparisons to their predecessor deflect attention and energy away from the real issues facing the business.

Successors' eventual success depends on their ability to use their own style (provided this conforms to good business practice). The employees are going to have to learn that successors have their own way of doing things. Successors have to assert themselves and excise their parents' ghost and, in the process, educate the organization that it needs to adjust and accommodate to their new style—not the other way around.

"I have to tell my dad to go to his room?" A final obstacle that children successors face is their inability to assert themselves against their parents. As children, they learned that parents were to be obeyed. Now comes this thing called succession, and suddenly they're the "parents" of the family business.

There will be times when successors take actions they know will run counter to their parents' preferences. So what do they do? Should they obey their parents and do things the way their parents would have? Or should they do things their own way?

Children successors must learn to convert their parents from parents into business peers. The parents are now an important constituency, but there will be times when the children successors will have to assert themselves and remind their parents that they are now in charge.

THE "PENALTIES" OF FOLLOWING A SUCCESSFUL PARENT

Following in the footsteps of one's parents can be challenging, and it is even harder when one's parents have been highly successful. These successors will face several difficulties that tend to pressure them into trying to mimic their parents' style. But remember, to achieve their own long-term success, successors must find and use their own personal style.

Asserting their own style is disloyal to their parent. There are certain internally imposed pressures to conform to the old ways.

When the successors were children, their parents seemed to have all the answers. And although this illusion may have been shattered by subsequent events, the initial belief remains. In addition, their parents did run the family business successfully, so the style they used must have been correct. It's logical for successors to wonder, "How can I possibly know more (or better) than they did?"

Thus, they are strongly tempted to try to imitate the style used by their parents, rather than doing things their own way.

All actions will be measured against the standard of "what their parents would have done." There are also externally imposed pressures to conform to the old ways.

The employees in the family business have a vested interest in that business's success. The way the predecessor did things helped to make the business successful, and they want the business to continue being successful. Any time successors take an action or make a decision that deviates from how their predecessor would have done it, they're immediately reminded "That's not the way your father would have done it."

These reminders of their predecessor's style serve to undermine any changes they may make. If they make a change and it's not successful, the entire organization will say: "We told you so!"

Continuing success will be attributed to their parents. If the business continues to be successful, people will believe that the continued success is the result of momentum created by the predecessors rather than anything done by the successor, thus undermining the successors' contributions. In addition, any setbacks will be attributed to the successors and will be evaluated harshly in the belief that not only did the successors make mistakes, but those mistakes were so serious that they changed the entire momentum of the business.

. . . And Others

Other baggage-related problems may also present themselves during succession.

PERSONAL CHALLENGES FACING MIDDLE-AGED SUCCESSORS

It's common for family business successors to inherit their role when they're middle-aged. If the parents want to retire at age sixty-five, by default their kids are probably in their early to mid forties. Although a nonfamily business might go out and hire a president in his mid fifties, family businesses are usually stuck with family members.

Middle-aged children usually have personal issues and challenges that have to be considered when choosing a successor.

Midlife is hard enough as it is . . . In middle age people notice little changes in their body and appearance: wrinkles, gray hairs, the fact that they can no longer bend over and touch their toes (in fact, they may not be able to see them).

But what happens when they look at their parents? This is most likely the time when their parents' health begins to fade. Since that's not a pleasant prospect, they can look at their children and find that their children either are coming of age or have entered adulthood. Things seem to be getting a little complicated.

Finally, since middle age is seen as the midpoint of a person's life, it often creates an overwhelming desire to understand one's purpose in life. People are continually struggling to answer the question "What's it all about?" Some prospective successors engage in irresponsible behavior; others withdraw into deep, introspective thoughts.

... and being the successor makes it that much tougher. The good news about being a successor is that you get a promotion. The bad news is that you have to work a lot harder than the nonsuccessors.

Middle age is the point in life when many successors face complicated personal issues. Successors find that they are hit with additional work demands at a time when they need to find greater balance in their life in order to resolve personal issues. This one-two punch amplifies any stress they might already feel.

Can the successor handle it? Succession planning must evaluate candidates' ability to manage these factors. Failure to investigate these issues may produce a successor who is destined to fail.

COMMON PROBLEMS FACING WIDOWS

Widows often struggle with a unique set of problems when their husbands die unexpectedly.

He "protected" her by keeping her in the dark. A lot of husbands have the strange notion that they're somehow protecting their wives by not bothering them with business concerns.

Although a husband's intentions may have been sincere, the result is a widow who does not have the knowledge or skills needed to run the family business.

This places her in a situation where she's entirely dependent upon advisors, be they long-term employees, outside lawyers or accountants, or her own children.

So why should the advisors be any better informed? If the widow was left in the dark, it's often true that her husband was withholding information from other people in the business as well. They might have known enough to do their respective jobs, but does anyone have enough information to see the big picture? It's possible that none of the advisors is sufficiently well informed to make solid business decisions.

There's an interesting dilemma here. The widow may know that she does not know how to run the business and that she's entirely dependent on these advisors. But since she's been excluded from business matters all these years, how is she able to judge the quality of the advisors she's dependent on? She can't. For example, one widow relied on her husband's key managers to keep their grocery store running, trusting them because they had been with her husband for almost thirty years. Unfortunately, she didn't realize that her husband had employed them because they were loyal and obedient, not because they were competent. Her husband had made all of the decisions and had single-handedly made the business successful. They loyally did their best, but they weren't up to the task. The store went out of business.

Sentimental feelings get in the way. Widows sometimes feel a sentimental urge to try to continue the family business. Sometimes the business serves as a tribute to her late husband; other times it's seen as a means by which to hold the remaining family members together. But is continuing the family business a viable option?

Unless the business has a strong group of managers or the children are ready to step in and continue, it's usually best for the widow to sell the business—and soon. If the widow herself tries to run the business or if she's forced to rely on an inept group of managers and would-be successors, the business will begin to falter and then fail. She would have received a much higher price selling it before it suffered from being ineptly run.

SUCCESSION DIFFICULTIES IN ENTREPRENEURIAL FAMILIES

Entrepreneurial families often face a unique set of difficulties. Sometimes the best way to describe succession in these families is to view it as a contest rather than as a process.

It's not a family, it's a competitive arena . . . Entrepreneurial founders are highly competitive people. Just look at what they've done: they had to successfully compete against—and overcome—tough odds to create a successful business. Unfortunately, these entrepreneurial founders tend to promote a family system that mirrors their own competitive traits. The result is a family system whose members view one another as rivals.

. . . complete with rivalries. The children may seek to undermine one another in numerous ways. Entrepreneur parents may avoid developing successors in order to maintain their own strength or seek to undermine their children's developmental activities. If all else fails, entrepreneurs may deliberately

foster rivalry among their children, maintaining their own power by pitting the children against one another.

A rivalry-plagued family system is not conducive to the cooperation needed to make succession successful.

13

....

Evolutionary Versus Revolutionary Succession

Every family business must achieve evolutionary succession. Even though evolutionary succession is something the family has to choose to perform, revolutionary succession is so potentially destructive to the business and painful to the people involved that it is not really an option.

Why the Distinction?

Evolutionary versus revolutionary is an approach that contrasts the extremes (i.e., the best-case versus the worst-case scenarios) in order to illustrate the differences. One benefit of this method is that it helps highlight the advantages of the preferred situation.

Evolutionary versus revolutionary is also a technique that evokes metaphors. "Evolution" connotes progress, improvement, strengthening. It can be viewed as an orderly process. "Revolution" is the opposite, filled with negative connotations. It can be violent, destructive, painful, chaotic—people can and do get hurt. The same is true with succession: it can be filled with the positive connotations of evolution or the negative consequences of revolution. The family has the power to determine which it will be.

Evolutionary succession has to be planned. It doesn't occur on its own. It may also be difficult to accomplish, especially if there's significant baggage in the family. If so, the family will need to bring in advisors. Although it may seem expensive to use advisors—which is why many family businesses don't—it's important to remember that if the family is carrying baggage and nothing is done, the eventual succession will be revolutionary and the price the business will pay for its revolutionary situation will far outstrip anything advisors will charge.

Revolutionary succession is the default mode, and it will occur if the business's owners sit back and do nothing. It's important to realize that succession is inevitable. People do not live forever, though a business organization can theoretically "live" forever. Since the organization has the potential to outlive the people in charge of it, mortality alone dictates that succession will be inevitable.

Whether the succession is evolutionary or revolutionary will affect the family's business along six key dimensions that are summarized in the accompanying table.

THE REASON FOR THE SUCCESSION

Succession occurs purely and simply because the people in charge of the business (who in family businesses are usually the owners) are departing and need to be replaced. So long as the business is in control of the process, it can take the necessary actions to pursue the best options.

Evolutionary. Evolutionary succession is internally driven, and the business itself controls the process. The business has

Evolutionary Versus Revolutionary Succession

Dimension	Evolutionary	Revolutionary
The Reason for the Succession	Succession is driven internally; the business is in control of the process, striving to maximize potential benefits.	Succession is imposed externally; the business is forced to react to events, striving to minimize potential damage.
Decision Making	Decisions are made after proper deliberation and evaluation of options.	Decisions are made in haste under unfavorable conditions.
Participation	All key stakeholders participate fully.	Few people are involved; the quality of their participation is questionable.
Development	Development activities are tailored to individuals' needs.	People sink or swim on their own; any training provided is generic and of marginal value.
Successor Selection	Selection is based on merit—the best potential successor is chosen.	Someone is chosen because he or she just happens to be available.
As Viewed by Outsiders	The process is seamless to outsiders.	Outsiders can see turmoil or other signs of distress.

the ability to minimize any problems succession might cause, and it also has the luxury to maximize the potential benefits. The most common cause of this type of succession is a desire by the owners to move on.

Revolutionary. Revolutionary succession is externally imposed on the business by outside events. The business does not control the process because it is forced to react to events. Quite simply, it finds that it's stuck with what it gets. Maximizing benefits becomes an exercise in minimizing the damage.

Revolutionary succession most commonly occurs because of the sudden death or disability of the owner. Even though this event is usually the catalyst for revolutionary succession, it need not be. If the organization has been implementing evolutionary succession, a death or disability may merely create a painful or rocky version of it, making very little impact upon the business.

DECISION MAKING

In a perfect world, businesses would get to make decisions by identifying what their objective is. Next, they would gather sufficient information, the key being that this information would have to be relevant. Third, they would determine all the available options. Fourth, they would carefully evaluate the pros and cons of each option; this assessment would be performed in an unbiased manner, using critical thinking. Finally, the business would select the option that best matched the original objective.

Ideally, a business is able to spend the appropriate amount of time going through these five steps. Some decisions are no-brainers—you race through them so fast that the process is nearly instantaneous. Other decisions are very complicated and require a significant amount of time to complete each step.

Because succession has such far-ranging implications for the family business, decisions should be made after carefully following the five-step process outlined above.

Evolutionary. In evolutionary succession, decisions are made after careful deliberation and a full evaluation of options. This is one of the key advantages of evolutionary succession: it enables the business to go through a proper decision-making process, thus increasing the chances of the business making correct decisions—ones that maximize the benefits to the organization.

It's important to note that businesses need to keep their decision-making process moving. People sometimes get confused and think that the more time they spend going through this process, the higher the quality of the decisions that are made. This is absolutely wrong. The key is to focus on the relevant and ignore the extraneous—not to let oneself get bogged down in analysis paralysis.

Also, it's important to remember that there's a cost involved in going through the decision-making process. Don't be lulled into a false sense that you can take all the time in the world to make decisions, because every minute you take to decide is costing you money.

Revolutionary. In revolutionary succession, decisions are often made in haste and with minimal thought because the business must take immediate action.

Being forced to react quickly brings several issues into the decision-making process: How do you know if you have sufficient information? Are your data accurate? Have you identified the options available to you? Do you understand the ramifications of each option? The reality is that most people are forced to make decisions with incomplete information.

In addition, the pressures of revolutionary succession may amplify the negative emotions and stresses that people experience, which often exaggerates any biases they have. As a result, they may misevaluate information, increasing the probability that bad decisions will be made.

PARTICIPATION

Having people participate in major business undertakings can create several benefits for the business. First, it improves communication. They know what's happening rather than being forced to rely on rumors. In addition, they know what they need to do to support the process. Second, it enables decision makers to obtain the information they need. No one has command of all the available information, so the owners need to involve the people who possess the relevant information. Third, it increases the chances that differing viewpoints will be presented. These differing viewpoints serve as a reality check and help prevent the danger of groupthink—the tendency of group members to stifle their own opinions, even when they know that the group is going to make a mistake, in order to promote harmony. Finally, it increases commitment to the decisions that are made and plans that are undertaken. Since people are given greater ownership, the chances of implementation and follow-through are increased.

Although allowing employees to participate in the succession process has clear benefits, it's important to remember that the goal is to involve the *key* people—those who will either play a significant role in implementing the plans that are made or who possess needed expertise. Involving too many nonkey people will overwhelm the process.

The business needs to utilize someone with strong facilitation skills to make the process effective. These seldom exist within a family business, so it's usually best to hire an outsider to help.

Evolutionary. All key stakeholders are full participants in the evolutionary succession process. In other words, the key people are involved.

In addition, because evolutionary succession occurs over time, people are able to participate in a way that does not disrupt their ability to perform their regular job.

Revolutionary. Revolutionary succession has minimal participation, usually limited to the surviving owner(s) and a small group of close advisors. These people need to react fast, and the process moves so quickly that there is seldom time to involve others. But there's no guarantee that this circle of close advisors has enough information to make good decisions.

Because of the crisis nature of revolutionary succession, key people are often too busy reacting to the crisis to be able to participate. And even if they're physically there and look as if they're participating, they may be too distracted by the overall situation to really participate.

DEVELOPMENT

People do not automatically possess the skills and knowledge needed to run their family's business. To be competent, successors need to learn about their company: its operations and the people working within it, its products, the industry, and so on. In addition, they need to have a sufficient understanding of general business principles. Finally, they need to possess leadership skills. Unfortunately, it takes time to gain this knowledge and perfect these skills, and all this learning has to occur while the successor performs his or her regular job.

In order to groom a successor properly, it's important to understand that person's strengths and weaknesses. This is accomplished by performing an assessment of that person and then formulating appropriate development activities. Since each person has a unique set of strengths and weaknesses, it's usually best to avoid a generic approach to development and instead formulate development activities in accordance with the individual's specific needs.

Evolutionary. Successors are identified well in advance of the actual succession, allowing significant work to be done developing them so they can step into their roles well prepared. They have sufficient time to pursue highly specific or customized activities that are the most effective way to meet their own individual development needs, thereby maximizing their growth. In addition, it's important to remember that people can *master* key lessons only if they've had sufficient time to absorb what they've been taught and to put their newly acquired skills into practice.

Revolutionary. Revolutionary succession tests the limits of its successors, who often find themselves in a sink-or-swim situation. Stress hinders people's learning abilities, and the successors are too overwhelmed to learn and master the skills they will need to be effective. Any training they may receive will probably focus on a hodgepodge of generic skills rather than the particular skills they need.

There's seldom a chance to perform a skills assessment, and failing to perform a proper assessment of successors' development needs means that they will not learn how to overcome the critical weaknesses that inhibit their effectiveness, since these deficiencies will not be uncovered or addressed by generic training activities.

SUCCESSOR SELECTION

Who will take over? Someone will have to be selected, yet there are numerous mistakes that families can and often do make.

The fundamental rule in selecting a successor is this:

> *The business (i.e., the family) must apply best business practices—no emotional or sentimental considerations are allowed. The best-qualified person gets the role of successor, but if no one in the family is qualified, an outsider must be brought in or the business must be sold.*

However painful the above seems, in the long run this maximizes *everyone's* benefits.

The process of determining the best qualified person to be successor starts by looking at the various candidates' strengths as well as their weaknesses. But this is not enough. The owners must also take a critical look at any baggage that is present. This factor is almost always overlooked, but it plays a critical role in determining whether a successor will be able to perform his or her role effectively.

Evolutionary. Evolutionary successors are carefully selected according to their merits. Because this is a careful and deliberate process, the owners should be able to take their time and evaluate the candidates carefully.

If no ideal candidates are found on the first pass, the owners can proceed to the next step: assessing the candidates' deficiencies and determining whether they can be overcome with sufficient training. The best potential successor is not necessarily the person who's currently the strongest. Rather, it's the person who can become the strongest over time.

Revolutionary. Revolutionary succession doesn't provide time to properly assess people's abilities before they're selected. The person selected to be successor is often the one who happened to be in the right place at the right time. The odds that the person who just happened to be there and who was selected is the best available candidate for the job are extremely low.

Assuming that the business survives the revolutionary succession, it is often faced with a thorny issue: How can it undo a selection that was made in haste? Problems will arise if the owner(s) later decides to come back and rectify the situation by installing someone more qualified.

SUCCESSION AS VIEWED BY OUTSIDERS

Who wants to do business with a business that's totally screwed up? It's too risky; it's much safer to go to a competitor that has its act together. People want to have confidence in their business partners.

But since succession in a family business is largely an internal matter, why should there be any concern with how the outside world views the succession process? Because if there is turmoil within the family's business, outsiders will detect it.

If the family business is to be sold, it's important that prospective buyers view it as a strong, healthy, viable entity. Any turmoil or chaos lessens the business's value, and buyers will prey upon these weaknesses in order to get the price down.

Even if the outside world does not perceive turmoil per se, there will be other signs that cause people to question whether they should continue to do business with the company. Examples of what outsiders will see are missed deadlines;

errors in work performed and delivered; things falling through the cracks; employees who seem stressed, frantic, or possibly irritable, and so on. These signal that a business is not able to meet customers' needs, and they will go elsewhere.

Evolutionary. Evolutionary succession is virtually undetectable to the outside world. The actual succession is such a calm process that people cannot tell it has happened. As a result, confidence in the business is generally maintained. If the business were to be sold, it would command a good price.

Revolutionary. The turmoil that accompanies revolutionary succession is readily apparent to customers and outside vendors, who often become concerned about the company's viability. The business will lose some of its customers due to these concerns.

Businesses experiencing revolutionary succession are often in a distressed state, which harms their ability to command a reasonable selling price. Everyone in the family loses.

The Dangers of Delaying (Failing) to Plan for Succession

Family businesses seem to have the mistaken notion that all that's needed to keep the business going is maintaining a perpetual stream of would-be successors.

Delaying or failing to plan for succession is the underlying cause of revolutionary succession. Delays reduce the options available to the business. The danger with reduced options is that they usually disappear in the order of their desirability— the first to go are those of most value to the business. If the family waits long enough, it won't want the options that are left.

MISSED OPPORTUNITIES THAT COULD PROVE FATAL

Succession is a rare opportunity for a family business to make critical strategic decisions. These have potentially far-ranging consequences that may benefit the business in many ways. Unfortunately, this opportunity is seldom recognized and less often capitalized upon. Family businesses that delay or fail to plan for succession always blow this one.

There is a series of steps companies can take during succession that will position the business for the future. Just as choosing the right successor perpetuates effective leadership in the business, these actions will perpetuate the business's viability in the marketplace.

Perform a strategic analysis. The business needs to look at its external environment and answer several key questions. Among these questions are: What is happening in our industry? What are our competitors doing? What will customers want from us in the future?

Answering questions like the ones above helps highlight key opportunities for the family business. It provides the owners with information about what the company should be doing in the future. New opportunities, products, and markets might be identified, allowing the business to grow. In addition, critical information may be obtained that indicates that what the family business is offering may not be wanted in the future, thus enabling the business to change its product offering and thereby remain viable.

Perform a critical self-analysis. Just as it looks outward into the external environment, the company should focus its attention on itself to identify its strengths and weaknesses. In so doing, the key is not to focus on the strengths and weaknesses of the present-day situation. Though this information is important and should be heeded, the real goal of this inquiry is to identify the business's strengths and weaknesses vis-à-vis its future needs as identified by the strategic analysis. In other words, what does the business need to do to capitalize on the opportunities that will be available to it in the future?

Identify the successor. Now knowing where the business should be headed and what weaknesses need to be overcome to get it there, the family is in a position to identify the successor. The question becomes: Who is best able to take the business where it needs to go? Rather than evaluating candidates with an eye as to who is best able to continue the business, the focus shifts to who is the best qualified to take the business where it needs to be.

The curse of the status quo successor. Businesses that fail to plan for succession find that they don't have time to go through the steps identified above before they install a new successor. If the owners failed to have the good judgment to think ahead and plan for succession, don't expect them to suddenly think in terms of identifying and capitalizing on new opportunities. Instead, they inevitably fall into the knee-jerk reaction of selecting successors who are best able to maintain the status quo. And why not? After all, these are the people who are usually the easiest to identify—they're often the best "yes men" within the company. But they are hardly the people who will be able to identify and exploit new opportunities.

Get out now. One advantage of performing a strategic analysis and a critical self-analysis is that it often provides the owners with an essential piece of information: that the family business is dying (i.e., that it will not be viable in the long run). This happens when the owners realize that the marketplace is evolving in a certain direction and the business does not have the ability to evolve along with it.

In such a situation, continuing the business means that it will decline, with a corresponding loss in value. Rather than installing a set of successors only to watch them fail through no fault of their own, the family should avoid succession altogether. In these situations, the best thing the family can do is sell its business—take the money and get out—before the value of the business declines and the family is left with nothing.

UNNECESSARY PAIN FOR EVERYONE—AND PLENTY OF IT TO GO AROUND

Not planning for succession forces people to endure problems that could have been avoided had actions been taken to ensure an evolutionary succession. This experience breeds resentment toward the people who failed to do the planning (i.e., the ones who caused the mess), contributes to strained relationships among coworkers, and spills over throughout the family.

Who can blame people for being resentful? They have had to scramble to adjust to the changes within the business, and they will have to continue to scramble to play catch-up for quite a while. They resent being forced to undergo this crisis.

14

·············

Successful Succession

There is a series of steps that family businesses can take that will help promote both a painless and a successful succession.

Guidelines for Succession Success

There are four critical guidelines that a family needs to follow when conducting succession.

Key Guidelines for Succession Success

- The best thing the family can do is put the best interests of the business first.
- Place merit ahead of family members' wishes when assigning jobs.
- Sell the business rather than let incompetent successors ruin it.
- Evolutionary succession must be used.

Guideline 1: The Family's Best Interest Is to Put the Best Interests of the Business First in Any Actions Taken or Decisions Made

Families seem to forget that the family business is what makes everything else possible. They fail to recognize that the business is the means that enables the family to pursue its own best interest. Putting the good of the business first has the effect of maximizing the family's financial resources, and in turn these resources give family members the ability to fulfill their needs and desires.

Family businesses must approach succession in a way that will maximize the value of their business. They will do this as long as each decision made or action taken is in conformance with this rule. Any time family-business owners put the family first, they weaken the business. If the business is profitable, it can survive an occasional deviation from this rule, but enough deviations will undermine it. Remember, a family business cannot be used as a tool to maintain family harmony.

Family baggage prevents people from thinking clearly during succession. It makes them want to use the business to help keep family members happy. They fear that applying good business practices and putting the best interests of the business first will create family conflict. It will, because people will yell and scream in direct proportion to the amount of baggage present. The fact that people are yelling and screaming reveals two very important things: first, there's baggage; second, the business is doing the right thing.

Guideline 2: Family Members Will Receive Jobs Based on Their Merit, Not According to Their Own Wishes

Succession creates openings in the business, and family members seem like the most logical people to put into these openings. But family members should get jobs in the business only if they have the skills to perform them *and* if there is a legitimate reason for those jobs to exist (i.e., the jobs support what the business is trying to achieve). If family members don't have the skills or if there's no reason for a position to exist, they don't get the job—period. Jobs are not to be created and given to family members because that's what they want.

Too often, successors use succession as an opportunity to indulge themselves and to pursue their own interests, demanding positions that sound interesting to them but for which they are completely unqualified. Many owners go ahead and employ their children, believing that this helps keep the family together, even though the children lack skills and may actually harm the business's viability. In such situations, it would make more sense to employ a competent outsider—thus maximizing the performance, profitability, and health of the family business—and using the additional profits to pay for alternative ways of promoting family togetherness.

Guideline 3: Owners Should Sell the Business Rather Than Let Incompetent Successors Ruin It

An owner looks around at the family members who could become successors. He has evaluated the capabilities of each of them in a very honest and objective manner and has come to the following conclusion: they just don't have it. What should the owner do? Sell the business.

Letting incompetent successors take over the family's business weakens it. As the company is weakened, its selling price drops. The weaker the company gets, the lower its selling price. Thus, the best time to sell a business is when it's still healthy.

If a family sells its business rather than letting it be taken over by incompetent family members, they would receive the maximum dollar value for it. The money received from this sale could be used as seed money to give the would-be successors the resources to pursue other interests. If they're truly inept, they'll surely find a way to blow this money as well, but at least they've been given the possibility of getting some value from the business.

Finally, it's important to remember that family members are not the only ones who will be hurt if incompetent successors take over and eventually destroy the family business; all the employees (and their families) will also be wiped out. Owners have an obligation to protect them as well.

Guideline 4: Evolutionary Succession Is the Only Acceptable Method of Succession

Evolutionary succession is a process that maximizes the opportunities that arise from succession. Families that work hard to prepare for succession are financially rewarded with a viable business or a large nest egg from the sale of it.

Failing to prepare for succession creates revolutionary succession. The business is forced to operate in a chaotic situation and must struggle to minimize the harm to itself. If it survives, it is seldom as viable or profitable as it might have been.

How the Big Boys Do It

Successful companies continually develop their people's skills. This includes training them for their current jobs, but, more important, it also involves preparing them to move up the career ladder.

There are four general requirements for a successful corporate succession planning system, and all four of them are applicable to family businesses. The key is to apply these requirements where and when appropriate.

THERE MUST BE A HIGH LEVEL OF CEO ATTENTION AND INVOLVEMENT

CEOs of successful corporations involve themselves personally in the succession process. They realize that it takes years to develop competent executives and are always searching for talented subordinates. In addition, they often have a board of directors that insists upon having a team of competent executives available should something happen to the current CEO.

The head of the business is the only person with the power to do it. Because of the obstacles inherent in succession planning, the head of the family business is the only person in a position to sponsor the succession. In other words, the business head is the only one with sufficient resources and power to push the process along to completion. His attention makes the succession a priority. Employees can tell when it's important to the owner, and if they're smart they'll make it a priority for themselves as well.

Subordinates have a vested interest in subverting one another. Another reason why succession planning requires owners' attention and involvement is that their subordinates can't be neutral, objective, or expected to cooperate with one another. After all, the would-be successors are likely to come from among these subordinates, so they're in competition with one another.

Each subordinate has a vested interest in trying to engineer the process so that he or she is selected as the successor. But the owner is the one who knows where these respective subordinates are headed and is the only person who can keep order.

THERE MUST BE A FORMAL MANAGEMENT DEVELOPMENT PROCESS

Competent successors don't become competent by chance—the business must make it happen.

Successful corporations provide extensive training for their employees. Some even require their senior managers to spend a minimum number of hours in training or educational programs each year. Training is provided through in-house trainers, by bringing in trainers from the outside, or by sending people to seminars and classes at the company's expense.

You've laid the groundwork if you're doing evolutionary succession. In evolutionary succession, considerable time is spent assessing the strengths and weaknesses of prospective successors, in formulating development plans to strengthen their skills, and finally in having them undergo the required activities so that they learn and master the required skills. The process of assessing the successors provides the owners with the information they need to implement development activities.

Flexible options are available. For a family business, a proper way to define "formal management development process" is to say that successors' development is part of a deliberate, purposeful process. This process may occur both within and outside of the family's business.

Within the family's business, there is a series of on-the-job activities that can help strengthen would-be successors. These activities include special assignments and projects to explore and resolve key problems, as well as preplanned job rotations to expand their perspective and develop their range of skills.

Outside the family's business, there is a series of formal learning programs that can complement the work-based learning activities. These include training programs and seminars, college courses, and leadership roles in volunteer organizations.

THERE MUST BE A BELIEF IN AND COMMITMENT TO THE PROCESS

Everyone has to be committed to the succession process. People at all levels are going to have to make sacrifices to see that it is properly performed and to reinforce one another's participation.

There may be too many distractions. The succession process is not easy. The would-be successors have their own full-time job responsibilities, plus all of the other family obligations. Now, in addition, they are expected to undertake management development activities. Only internally driven motivation—a belief in and commitment to this process—will sustain them as they make the extra effort.

Faking it isn't limited to sex. Would-be successors who aren't committed will take short cuts to circumvent the management development process. They will find that they are too busy to do what they're supposed to, but will make it appear as though they're complying by merely going through the motions. The effect is that they're not being properly trained to assume leadership in succession.

One danger with succession planning is that the only way to tell its effectiveness is after the fact—when it is too late to train the successors. Would-be successors need to remember that they have no choice but to be committed to the succession process. If the succession is not successful and the company subsequently fails, they don't just lose their jobs—they lose their estates.

EXECUTIVES MUST BE EVALUATED BASED ON THEIR ABILITY TO DEVELOP MANAGERS

A key activity of all managers is development of their subordinates. In large companies, managers and executives are given yearly goals for developing their subordinates (i.e., potential successors) and are evaluated and rewarded based upon how well they perform this function. Linking goals for successor development into the performance evaluation process is a method companies can use to help enforce compliance.

The polarity must be reversed. Many family businesses aren't large enough to institutionalize this top-down requirement. They are, however, in a position to reverse the orientation and impose it upon the successors themselves.

The formal management development process then becomes a part of all would-be successors' yearly goals. The specific courses they will take or the special projects they will perform are clearly identified, along with the reason the activity is being undertaken. Each would-be successor has a clear road map of what he or she is expected to do over the next year.

Would-be successors are still getting an allowance. At the end of the year, would-be successors should be evaluated on how well they complied with their development activities. If they did well, they should be given a favorable review in this area and rewarded for it. Think of this as an adult version of giving them their allowance in return for their performing certain chores.

A Three-Part Test to Apply to Prospective Successors

How do you decide who the successor will be? Several family members (usually the owner's children) want the job, but only one of them will get it. Since the kids who are not picked are going to be angry, can anything help ensure that the person selected will be an effective successor?

The following three-part test will help evaluate successor candidates. Each part acts as a screen to help filter out people who will not be successful. The people who are deciding upon the successor—be they the owners, outside advisors, whoever—should apply this test when reviewing the candidates.

A Three-Part Test to Apply to Prospective Successors

	YES	NO
Do they have the skills, abilities, and competence?	___	___
Do they have full authority (or can they get it)?	___	___
Is this what they want to do?	___	___

"No" to any of the above is a disqualifier.

PART 1: DO THEY HAVE THE SKILLS, ABILITIES, AND COMPETENCE TO DO THE JOB?

This is the question that everyone asks. It requires a critical examination of the person's abilities. Unfortunately, there is no universal test that can be given to candidates to help determine who's best qualified. The person picking the successor needs to rely upon his or her own best judgment.

Candidates must be evaluated with the correct orientation and perspective. Two common mistakes are made during the evaluation process. The first is a failure to look for the best *potential* successor—the one who will, over time, possess the strongest skills. This may not be the person who is strongest today; rather, it's the person who will grow into the strongest. The second is a failure to evaluate the candidates in terms of where the business should be headed in the future, rather than where it is today. The status quo successor is the easiest to spot, which makes him or her the easiest to pick but not the best choice.

It's usually a photo finish. When "Do they have the skills, abilities, and competence?" is the only question that is asked, several of the prospective successors may be judged to be of equal ability. How do you choose one from among equals?

Proceeding to the next two questions in this three-part test will reveal differences between the candidates and enable the decision maker to make the correct selection. Ironically, these questions are usually not asked.

PART 2: DO THEY HAVE FULL AUTHORITY (OR CAN THEY GET IT)?

A successor must have full authority to perform his job, and this is not something that occurs automatically. Therefore, a critical trait is needed by a successor: the ability to enforce his or her authority. Since each of the prospective successors is unique, it's likely that one of them will possess this trait to a greater extent than the others.

"They're riding back into town, and no one will help me." Any of three common scenarios can cripple a new successor. The first is when the predecessors either don't let go of or don't remove themselves from the business. The second is when the siblings who were not selected continue to battle for control or meddle in one another's activities. The third is when the people within the business cannot accept the new power structure—they may have worked for the predecessor so long that they can't accept the fact that this person has departed.

All these scenarios prove that the successor is not automatically in charge. The new successor may have to flex his or her muscles and enforce the succession—and may have to do so all alone.

Sometimes you've got to go out and shoot a few bad guys to make a statement. If successors do not have full authority, they must be willing to fight to get it, and continue to fight until they do. I often refer to this as the Clint Eastwood method of enforcing authority.

The second half of the question—*"(or can they get it)"*—determines whether candidates have the psyche to be the successor. If they are not willing to fight to impose their new role on the organization, they won't succeed. Instead, they will be overwhelmed by the organization and its baggage. For example, in one garment company, the youngest brother bought the business from his parents. Unfortunately, even though he was now the owner, he was not willing to fight to assert himself against his brother and sister, who continued to do whatever they wanted. The company failed because his brother's and sister's actions counteracted each other and the business could not meet its delivery deadlines.

PART 3: IS THIS WHAT THEY WANT TO DO?

Successors often fall into their role out of a sense of obligation, and family businesses must take steps to prevent this from occurring.

"Distance" is necessary. It's important to step back and evaluate prospective successors in terms of whether they ever achieved distance from the family. Achieving distance is the only way these children could have discovered themselves, to learn who and what they are, what their true calling is, what they really want to do. Only once they've attained distance do many of them discover that their family's business is not for them.

The successful candidate must have a burning desire to do the job. Candidates need to gauge the extent of their desire. Do they have a burning desire? Taking over a family business is a difficult task, and only a strong desire will sustain a person through this challenge.

Overcoming Personal Obstacles to Developing Successors

There are a number of reasons why business owners fail to develop competent successors; these are often the result of personal attributes or misinformation.

A LACK OF COACHING SKILLS

Owners are often talented businesspeople. Their skills and abilities include creating and growing a business. Developing a successor, on the other hand, requires the talents of a mentor or a coach.

Coaching involves the ability to identify a person's strengths and weaknesses, formulate a set of development activities that will preserve the strengths and correct the weaknesses, and give honest and useful feedback. There's also the need for an occasional pep talk. Many business owners lack these skills.

Owners do not have to be another Knute Rockne. But they must view themselves as people who help others develop their abilities. Everyone who works in the business is on their team, and they seek to help each employee master the game.

PREFERRING TO WORK ON IMMEDIATE PROBLEMS THAT PRODUCE QUICK RESULTS

A business presents a never-ending barrage of problems that must be addressed immediately. Thus, owners have a built-in bias toward taking action and seeing quick results.

Developing a successor is a slow, time-consuming process that runs counter to this short-term orientation. Many owners just don't have the patience to engage themselves in long-term projects. Who can blame them? By jumping in and handling urgent problems, they get instant gratification. Better yet, they get all the credit. It might take a decade or more before the successor they helped groom begins to demonstrate his or her competence. Plus, it's the successor who is then successful and gets all the credit, while the person who coached the successor has been long forgotten.

A BELIEF THAT DEVELOPMENT ACTIVITIES ARE TOO COSTLY

Family-business owners often think of developing their children in terms of sending them to expensive colleges or costly training programs. But it's not just the dollars that are spent on tuition or training that are important, the cost of that person's time is important as well. Will the owners need to pay someone else to do the job while their kid is off learning? Many families simply cannot afford such an investment.

The family might also consider on-the-job development activities (i.e., special projects or frequent job rotation) but be forced to reject these because their business can afford to employ only people who are able to perform at their full ability. Putting people into various jobs to learn is viewed as forcing the business to bear the burden of carrying deadweight while the would-be successors learn.

I understand owners' concerns about development being costly. They're right. But how much will it cost the business if the successors fail?

FALSE OPTIMISM BASED ON PAST SUCCESSES

Family-business owners shift back and forth between fear and optimism in ways that create a weird paradox. They're continually fearful of the future and the challenges it may bring, and this is good—it's realistic. And although they are continually frightened, they tend to be optimistic about the ability of their business to rise up and meet these challenges. Their business's past successes have created a belief that things will somehow work out.

Unfortunately, they're setting the stage for revolutionary succession. But as with every other challenge their business has faced, they believe that succession can be handled when it arises and there's simply no need to spend energy on developing successors.

A FEELING THAT THEY'LL BE DISPENSABLE ONCE THEY'VE DEVELOPED A SUCCESSOR

"Let me get this straight. You want me to make myself dispensable?" This is the view many owners have toward developing successors. Technically, they may be right, because developing successors means creating people who will be capable of performing the role that is now being performed by the owner.

Many owners fear that they will be seen as dispensable once their chosen successors are capable of performing the functions they currently perform. But in fact, developing successors is not the same as becoming replaceable; instead, it's like buying insurance to protect your nest egg.

Steps to Help Children Enter the Family Business

When the children begin working in the business, it's often the first step along the path to their becoming successors. How they enter the business can have a large impact on their ability to eventually take it over.

TEACH THE KIDS THAT THEY WILL NEED TO EARN RESPECT FROM THE ORGANIZATION

Children often enter their parents' business with a bad misperception that can create problems for them when working with nonfamily employees.

What makes you so special? Children entering the family business often feel that it's their automatic right to be respected by the people in the organization. After all, it's their family's business and these people work for the family. They're partially right; it *is* their family's business, but what this really means is that it's their parents' business, not theirs.

Where did they get this feeling of entitlement? Yes, they're entitled to the same amount of respect any other person deserves, but they did not make the business what it is, their parents did.

You want respect . . . earn it. The fastest way of creating resentment among employees is for the kids to enter the business with an "attitude."

The kids entering the business need to do so with a very unassuming attitude and show respect for others. This means having good interpersonal skills and conduct, and it's something their parents should have taught them.

The kids must also work hard and do their jobs competently. They must learn about the business and perform their jobs just like any other employee. In addition, the owners must make it very clear throughout the organization that their kids will be held accountable, just like any other employee.

TELL THE ORGANIZATION THAT THE KIDS ARE GOING TO BE COMING IN

The kids' entry into the business can easily create tension within the organization. People often feel intimidated because they don't know what these kids—who will very likely be successors—are like.

Giving advance warning to the employees helps to desensitize them to the children's arrival. Employees should not be surprised by the kids showing up unexpectedly, carrying a briefcase. Instead, the children should be taken around and introduced to them. These steps, if coupled with the right attitude on the part of the kids, will help to put the employees at ease.

TELL YOUR CHILDREN WHAT YOU KNOW ABOUT THE EMPLOYEES

Owners often have a good feel for the individual strengths and weaknesses of their employees; they've worked with some of these people for years.

Share what you think you know. What little nuances about employees can owners tell their kids that will help them be more effective? What are the employees' styles, preferences, strengths, weaknesses? How can the kids interact with the employees to help all of them do their best? Owners should share this information with their kids to help get them up to speed.

But remember that it's only your opinion. Although this information can be helpful, the children must be encouraged to come to their own conclusions regarding the employees' capabilities. It's possible the owner is wrong and their kids will enter the business misinformed. Also, remember that the nature of the relationships is different. Employees will be interacting with the owners' kids—not the owners themselves—and they will view them differently. This means that they will react to them differently. The information owners share may be correct vis-à-vis themselves but be off base for their kids.

TREAT EVERYONE FAIRLY

A lot of the resentment employees direct toward the owners' children who enter the business stems from assumptions that these kids will get preferential treatment. The best way to prevent this is to treat everyone fairly. Within a family business, treating everyone fairly means treating everyone equally when it comes to business matters.

"Fairly" = "equally" vis-à-vis performance expectations. The owners' children need to be treated just like every other employee—neither too harshly nor too leniently.

How can a family business treat everyone fairly? By clearly defining and enforcing performance expectations. Everyone must be held equally responsible for meeting goals and deadlines, for following rules, when it comes time to receive performance reviews, and so forth. While there's no way to treat everyone with 100 percent equality, an owner can act most fairly by striving to set and adhere to a uniform set of standards.

What employees don't know won't help the owners. But just doing this—holding people equally accountable—isn't enough, because there's no guarantee that employees know it's happening. Owners must take the next step and make sure that everyone in the business knows that everyone will be treated equally. There's no benefit in doing so if employees don't know it's being done, because people will tend to assume otherwise.

AVOID PLAYING FAMILY AT WORK

Family members may find it too easy to reenact family roles within the business. Though they don't intend to, this can have the unintended consequence of reminding employees that they're not part of the family.

Don't reinvent the caste system. Playing family at work can create a caste system within the business, with family members being on the top and employees at the bottom. To prevent a caste system from emerging, any talk about family matters or activities should be kept to an absolute minimum and should not be done in front of nonfamily employees.

When at work, act like employees. While at work, and especially in front of nonfamily employees, any interactions among family members should conform to people's respective business-system roles. For example, the kids must treat their parents as the boss and not as their parents—Daddy's little girl can't try to dodge out of a missed deadline by acting cute just as she would have at home when she forgot to do a chore.

Tips to Help Get Rid of Mom and Dad

Owners often pose objections when the time to implement succession arrives. One of the most common objections is that the owner lacks confidence in the successor's abilities.

The reality is that confidence in the successor's ability is seldom the real reason an owner refuses to leave. No, other things are going on here, and these issues are what need to be addressed.

DYLAN THOMAS REVISITED

The children have become convinced that the Dylan Thomas poem cited at the beginning of this part was written with their parents in mind. They've done all the hard work to develop themselves as competent successors. The parents keep saying they want to retire, but for various reasons they just won't go. Expectations have been raised, and there's going to be conflict unless and until the parents step aside.

When does life begin? There's an old joke that goes as follows: Three people were asked to answer the question "When does life begin?" The first person answered, "At conception." The second person said, "No, at birth." The third person disagrees: "You're both wrong. Life begins when the kids move out and the damn dog dies." This is the perspective the parents need to adopt.

The family business is often the parents' nest egg, so it's critical that it be protected. The best way to protect it is for the parents to step aside as their children are entering their prime. In addition, as mentioned earlier, certain personal issues are inherent in working so closely with a business—it creates the person's identity. But if the business has been faithfully doing the hard work of evolutionary succession, the parents must step aside.

The Lizzie Borden school of succession. As a final warning to parents, I have to remind them of the following reality: if the kids want you out, they'll find a way. One way or another, you'll get the ax. It doesn't matter how illogical, irrational, or destructive their actions, they will do whatever it takes to get you out of the business, even if it means destroying the business itself.

Another ugly reality is that the kids have a lot less to lose than their parents. They're younger and stronger. While the parents will be wiped out if the kids destroy everything, the kids still have a long time to rebuild their lives and recover from any mess they make. For example, in one printing company, the father said that the only way he'd retire was when sales stopped growing. His son, in an effort to force his dad to retire, deliberately began to antagonize key clients. Several of these clients became unhappy and took their business elsewhere. These were large accounts, and there weren't other large companies to replace them. The family's business shrank to only half its former size and no longer had sufficient revenues to be profitable.

GRADUATED RETIREMENT AND SUCCESSION

An evolutionary technique that can ease both the outgoing owners and their children into their new roles is called "graduated retirement and succession." In this, the outgoing owners begin to take increasingly longer vacations prior to retirement. It's a series of dress rehearsals for the real thing.

It benefits the parents. The outgoing owners have an opportunity to prepare for a new role for themselves by using their time during the extended vacations to explore new interests. The last thing they need is to wake up one morning and not go into work for the first time in forty years.

It can also help to ease the outgoing owners' mind by allowing them to see that the business can function in their absence (or maybe this is their worst nightmare come true).

It benefits the children. The successors will benefit because this process gradually eases them into their new role. They experience increasing levels of responsibility with the advantage of knowing that their parents will be returning and available to resolve any problems they can't. This provides an opportunity for them to build their confidence as well as demonstrate their competency to the rest of the organization.

The gradual nature of this process helps to avoid the danger of the successors feeling overwhelmed. Remember, they're usually at a stage in life when they're already struggling with other issues. There's no benefit in making succession any more difficult than it has to be.

PART IV

··

It Comes with the Territory

··

Other Problems Inherent in Family Businesses

There are certain difficulties that present themselves in family businesses just because the business is a family business, regardless of whether or not there's any family baggage. As always, the secret is to identify the problem's origin. The solutions are often straightforward.

15

·············

They've Stayed Too Long at the Fair: Long-Tenured Managers and Employees

An interesting characteristic of family businesses—more than of other types of businesses—is that they often have a group of long-tenured managers and employees.

Is It My Imagination, or Have They Been Here Forever?

Family businesses often view their employees as members of their extended family. There are times when this can be a real plus for a business, for instance when it results in a genuine feeling of concern for the workers.

But viewing employees as extended family also has its drawbacks. For instance, it may be just as difficult to fire them as it is to fire bona fide family members. Instead of making business decisions based on objective standards, emotional considerations come into play. The owners are not applying good business standards, expectations, or judgment.

NEVER CAN SAY GOOD-BYE

Family businesses have a strong dislike of turnover among their managers and key long-term employees. This is because the departure of a manager or employee with long tenure often creates burdens for family members. Rather than these departures being viewed as an inevitable part of business, they are viewed as creating mini–family crises.

There'll be more work for the rest of us. A departing manager or long-tenured employee leaves behind a workload that must be carried by the remaining employees. This is particularly significant when the business is small and there aren't many workers left to absorb the work. Also, the departing person probably possessed institutional knowledge that enabled him or her to do the job more efficiently than the people taking over the work. As a result, it will probably take longer for others to do the job.

It's also possible that the departing employee didn't perform his or her work correctly but had somehow managed to hide the fact. Not only will the remaining employees be forced to do the work, they'll have the additional burden of cleaning up the mess that was left behind.

Training and/or retraining will be needed. Eventually, the departing employee will be replaced with a new person, who is probably going to have to be trained. Other people will have to be patient while this new person is learning the job.

Who's going to train this new person? You guessed it: the remaining employees, who have already been burdened with the excess work left by the departing employee.

An "outsider" will enter the business family. Remember, the long-tenured person who has departed was probably viewed as a member of the extended family, and the replacement will often come from outside the company. The replacement is thus an outsider. In addition to concerns about the new person's competence, there is an additional concern about whether or not he or she will fit into the family.

SO, HOW DO WE PREVENT THESE "BURDENS"? BY CREATING NEW ONES!

Family businesses often overpay long-term managers and key employees in an effort to retain them. This practice has two consequences.

Resources are wasted. Overpaying people wastes resources that could be used elsewhere. This can be particularly cumbersome when the business is small and lacks deep pockets. It is a formula for trouble when a business does not have the money to make infrastructure investments (e.g., in new equipment to expedite its operations, employee training to strengthen skills and performance) that would increase its efficiency, profitability, and chances of overall success because it is overpaying long-tenured employees.

A status quo orientation is promoted. Long-tenured managers and employees have a tendency to try to maintain the status quo. After all, they've become just as comfortable with the way things are as the owners are. Bringing new people into the business often means that changes will be made, or at least attempted. Overpaying someone to stay in place is considered a good investment to avoid having to bring new people—potential troublemakers—into the company. Unfortunately, maintaining the status quo can be dangerous for a business operating in today's rapidly changing environment.

THE DANGERS OF LONG-TENURED MANAGEMENT

Experienced managers can be valuable, especially when their job forces them to grow continually. Unfortunately, what is learned in family businesses is often just how to hang around. Over time, many family businesses build up a core group of long-tenured managers who have developed a pack mentality. They have found that it's far easier to maintain the facade that they're a big extended family and not rock the boat, rather than to look out at the rapidly changing marketplace and try to adapt to it. Instead of being a seasoned management team with valuable experience, such people are dangerous to the business's existence.

Shared experiences breed a homogeneous mentality. Managers with a long history of common experiences tend to have similar beliefs, values, and attitudes. They may also be about the same age. They've spent years, possibly decades, in an environment that reinforces their collective outlook. This group's motto is often best summed up as follows: "We're open to any new ideas that conform to our preconceived expectations."

If this is carried to extremes, the group members will actively perpetuate the problem by acting as their own screening device. Any ideas that depart from the consensus will be avoided because they will cause discomfort for fellow group members. Harmony among the management team must be maintained.

It is dangerous for a company to have a management group that is not open to new ideas, innovations, or change.

Risk aversion increases. Long-tenured managers often have a short time until retirement. Thus, they do not want to do anything to jeopardize their financial situation. They have spent most of their lives working for the family business and are largely dependent upon it for their pensions, retirement funds, and so on. Actions that focus on building the business or repositioning it in the marketplace inherently carry risk. Not all such actions will be successful, and the business may even experience setbacks.

There's nothing wrong with being risk averse, per se. But the reality is that the market is continually changing and appropriate responses to its changes are prudent. When risk aversion becomes an obstinate insistence on preserving the status quo, the business is put at risk. A business can preserve itself into extinction.

Retirements may occur en masse. Since they all tend to be about the same age, long-tenured management groups often retire around the same time.

We've already discussed the problems that arise when a single person departs the company. Can you imagine the effect when the whole management group does so in rapid succession?

Someone else's seniority may create obstacles for successors or other agents of change. Long-tenured managers may be entrenched in old habits and unwilling to change. This can be especially troublesome when succession has occurred or when a younger group of managers has been brought in to try to effect change.

Long-tenured managers will seek to reenforce the predecessors' past practices, since these are what have carried the organization to where it is. Successors will be pressured to conform to the old style instead of being supported while they implement new styles and practices. In addition, successors are often younger in age and experience than the long-tenured management team. Some of these managers may have been working in the business before the successors were even born, and it can be hard for the younger people to assert themselves against the older ones. The idea of respect for one's elders then takes on a diabolical twist.

Obstacles to and Dilemmas in Discharging Long-Tenured Employees

Sometimes the best interests of the business suggest that certain individuals should be terminated. Unfortunately, family-business owners may find that they are unable to clean house for a number of reasons and must instead carry deadwood (a form of carrying baggage).

THEY'VE LEARNED THEIR BAD HABITS FROM YOU (BUT AT LEAST YOU WERE A GOOD TEACHER)

The paternalistic leadership style common in many family businesses tends to create employees of marginal ability. Owners, acting as "parents," tend to do things and make decisions for employees rather than forcing them to take the initiative. In such cases, it's better to be a loyal, obedient employee (or is that a loyal, obedient child?) than to be assertive.

Family-business owners also have a bad habit of keeping people in the same job too long. This is often simply the result of the business being small—there aren't any other jobs. Unfortunately, staying in the same role over an extended period of time has a tendency of further narrowing an employee's job skills.

The result of this one-two combination is a group of people who are loyal to the family but are marginal performers.

AND YOU'VE REWARDED THEM FOR IT

I've already discussed how long-term employees are often overpaid as a reward for their loyalty. These same employees also tend to adopt a lifestyle that matches their income—one that is beyond what they could afford if they were being paid market rates.

Unfortunately for these long-tenured employees, their lack of readily marketable job skills (caused by an overly narrow job focus coupled with the learned trait of minimal self-initiative) combined with a salary that is inflated beyond what the market pays tends to make them unemployable elsewhere.

HOW CAN YOU CLEAN UP A MESS YOU'VE MADE (AND STILL BE ABLE TO LOOK AT YOURSELF IN THE MIRROR)?

Owners wishing to strengthen their business find that they are unable to clean house for three very significant reasons.

Et Tu, Brute? Inherent in family businesses is a strong sense of tradition and loyalty. It's a value employees believe in. To dismiss long-term employees would be to betray the family's commitment or obligation to them.

More Brutal than the LAPD with Rodney King. The fact that these employees are often unemployable elsewhere exacerbates the pain associated with terminating them. This goes beyond the callousness of corporate downsizing—at least downsized employees may have marketable skills and probably weren't overpaid.

Parental Control Isn't Just Limited to "976" Numbers. An interesting dynamic often comes into play if the successors decide they want to clean house. The fastest way to incur the wrath of the parents and to have them interject themselves back into the business is to try to terminate long-tenured managers or employees.

These employees are often considered untouchable because the predecessors have a strong bond to them. They've been loyal to the family for many years. Successors wishing to clean house are often forced to choose between doing what's right for the business and doing what makes their parents happy. For example, I've seen many instances where a successor wanted to replace old Joe, the plant foreman. Joe is an old friend of his father, has been at the company for years, and his main function was to be a good fishing buddy for Dad. The successor knows that if he or she tries to replace old Joe, he or she will receive an angry visit from Mom and Dad to tell them this is not allowed. Sometimes, parents have even fired their kids!

WHERE SHOULD "DEADWOOD" BE CLASSIFIED ON THE BALANCE SHEET: AS AN ASSET OR A LIABILITY?

Family-business owners are often forced to bear the burden of carrying deadwood in their organization. They're stuck trying to operate a business where they lack employees who can do the work effectively, the financial resources to hire replacements, and the freedom to make business decisions without damaging familial relationships.

16

·············

Interlopers, Consorts, and Other Undesirable Meddlers

Everything might be okay if people would just leave the owners alone and let them go about running their family's business. But just like ants, there is a cast of characters that shows up to spoil the family's picnic.

Inheritors

Let's assume that the business owners have done a reasonable job of planning for succession. No matter how orderly it appears the process will be, the business is still not out of danger. Enter the inheritors, who have the uncanny ability to disrupt an otherwise orderly succession process. They do this for three reasons.

THEY WANT TO DECIDE WHAT THEY WILL INHERIT

Inheritors somehow feel that they are supposed to have the right to decide what they inherit: a specific amount of money, particular pieces of property, the form of ownership in the family's business. The intensity of this belief seems to increase in direct correlation with the imminence of their receiving their inheritance. Had this fight arisen years earlier it would have been less intense and more manageable, but coming at the eleventh hour it is very disruptive.

THEIR IDEA OF "FAIR" MAY CAUSE CONFLICT

Inheritors will tell you that what they want is for everyone to be treated fairly, when what they're really saying is that they want to be treated fairly. But are their perceptions of what's fair shared by others? To make matters worse, the conflict is over a limited set of assets. By definition, one person's gain must translate into another's loss.

There's no guarantee that what the inheritors believe is a fair arrangement is in the business's best interests. Even in situations where the inheritors are in agreement, do they understand the implications of what they're seeking? They may actually be sowing the seeds of future disagreements, such as when all inheritors insist upon equal amounts of ownership and control even though only a few of them will actually be involved in running the business.

FIGHTS WILL BE EMOTIONALLY BASED

Fights among successors tend to be emotionally based, usually stemming from each one's feeling of entitlement. Emotionally based fights tend to be fought with a particularly destructive intensity. Oftentimes the conflict is based upon old rivalries or unresolved issues from childhood. Finally, because these fights are fought in the Zone of Mortal Combat, cold, clear logic seldom resolves the problem.

In-Laws and Spouses

In-laws and spouses who enter or interject themselves into the business present a series of problems—for the business, for the family members, for the in-laws themselves.

You will note that I'll be using the terms "in-law" and "spouse" interchangeably, but the discussion below is limited to spouses. It is also possible for extended in-laws (i.e., relatives of the spouse) to come into the business, which amplifies the problems discussed in this section.

IT'S ALL CONTINGENT UPON SLEEPING WITH SOMEONE

This is the main premise of this section. Maybe it's a little blunt, but it makes the point.

It isn't considered sexual harassment in these situations. First and foremost, these people have their jobs because they're sleeping with someone. Unlike their coworkers who were born into the family, in-laws achieved their position through marriage.

Continuing employment in the family business may be a tenuous proposition. Since their job is one of the fringe benefits of the marriage, their continued position is often dependent upon a continuing marriage. Divorce and a pink slip are intertwined.

Why can't we divorce you instead of the person you married? Divorce represents formal removal from the family system. It should also represent formal removal from the business system (if these systems are healthy). There's no reason to believe that a person should want his or her ex-spouse to continue working for the family's business, and that person's ongoing presence will serve as a continual reminder of the failed marriage. But does the rest of the family see it that way?

There are times when the other family members view the ex-spouse as a valuable employee and resent having to replace him or her. In fact, it's not uncommon for the rest of the family to like the ex-spouse better than their own blood relative. This sets the stage for conflict with the blood relatives who don't think that their stake in the business should be forced to suffer by having to replace a valuable contributor.

DE-FACTO SECOND-CLASS CITIZENSHIP

Even though in-laws are technically members of the family, there's no getting around the fact that they achieved this status through marriage rather than blood. Members of the blood family often view only themselves as the "true" family. They may resent the emergence of an in-law who wields significant control in the business. This resentment may be acted out in petty conflicts or through attempts to sabotage the in-law. Either of these has a harmful effect on the business.

In many ways, in-laws have more in common with long-tenured or trusted employees than they do with the rest of the family. They're part of the family, but the extended family rather than the true family.

CONFLICTING LOYALTIES

In-laws have loyalties to three different entities. What happens when these loyalties present conflicting demands?

To their spouse. What happens when the in-law's spouse is fighting with parents or other family members? The question:

Who does the in-law support? The answer: At the end of the day he or she has to sleep with his or her spouse.

To the business. In theory, in-laws working for the family business have a duty to use their judgment and take actions that place the best interests of the business first. But what happens when in-laws disagree with the rest of the family? They'll feel pressured to espouse viewpoints and take actions that are not consistent with what they believe. It is hard, if not unfair, to expect in-laws to disregard these pressures when they may feel like (and actually be) second-class citizens.

To themselves. What happens when people marry into a family that strongly expects them to enter the family's business? Is this a marriage, or is the family drafting college athletes into the farm team?

Ultimately, for spouses to be happy they must seek employment in a vocation and by an employer of their choosing, especially if they have no real desire to work in the family business.

AGITATORS

It's one thing to be loyal to one's spouse. That's expected. But what if an in-law is a troublemaker? Usually the family system has achieved harmony prior to this spouse's arrival. There is a clear-cut set of expectations, and people have learned their roles in both the family and business systems. Enter the spouse who sees things differently.

New spouses have an uncanny ability to enter the family system (and indirectly the business system) and suddenly feel that their husband or wife is getting the short end of the deal. The impact on the family business is disruptive as new spouses complain that their husband or wife is entitled to more—more power, more compensation, a greater share in the profits. Sometimes they're right, but often they're just greedy.

The family has a dilemma: Should they try to placate newly arrived and greedy spouses, or should they draw boundaries and try to control them? The spouses who married the newly arrived in-laws also faces this dilemma, only it's more intense.

Nonemployed Spouses

Even though both the husband and wife may not work together in the business, barring some type of legal arrangement they're both owners. So no matter how far removed they are, nonemployed spouses still exert an influence on the business.

SPOUSES HAVE A GREATER IMPACT THAN YOU MAY THINK

Even if spouses are not involved in the family business, they have a significant impact. For example, employees may fear them if they visit the business unexpectedly. What happens if the spouse sees people talking in the hallway? Will nonemployed spouses snitch on employees to their husband or wife? What if the reason the employees were standing around was because they were taking a five-minute break after having worked through lunch to meet a tough deadline?

GUIDELINES FOR MINIMIZING PROBLEMS

Certain things should be done to help mitigate unintended problems.

Limit nonemployed spouses' presence at and interaction in the family business. Remember that spouses do have an impact that may have unintended consequences. A good way of preventing this is simply to limit their exposure to the business. Let spouses visit only when there's a good reason, and let the employees know in advance that they'll be there.

Spouses should act as emissaries of goodwill when they are present. Spouses should be sincere and show a genuine interest in the employees. After all, the employees are the ones who make the business money. But a spouse's attitude must be sincere; employees can tell if it's an act.

Nonemployed spouses shouldn't make the mistake of trying to be the employees' best friend. It is a business, after all. The owners might have to ask employees to do difficult things in the course of their employment; the fact that a nonemployed spouse is a close friend might make carrying out these requests difficult.

Don't meddle or tell tales. If nonemployed spouses see things that are of concern, they should mention it to their spouse. But this should be done only if they are certain that they fully understand the situation.

Don't let employees play spouses against each other. Be wary when employees approach nonemployed spouses with requests, rather than the ones who are working in the business. Nonemployed spouses don't want to summarily rebuff employees who bring issues directly to them, because they may have good reasons for doing so. The key is to determine whether they're trying to play the spouses off against each other.

Don't view employees as personal servants. Leona Helmsley was hardly a role model for building employee morale. Expecting employees to perform servantlike tasks destroys morale.

It is inappropriate to ask employees to do little favors, because they're not really in a position to refuse. For example, nonemployed spouses should think twice before bringing in their daughter's Girl Scout cookies order sheet. However innocuous it may seem, do the employees really have a chance to say no?

2nd (and 3rd and 4th . . .) Wives

Someday this section will need to be retitled "husbands and wives" instead of simply "wives." But we're talking about events that were often set in motion years, if not decades, ago, when business was a male-dominated arena.

JEALOUSY

Many kinds of jealousy may arise, and each one impacts the business.

Of their spouse's kids. Can owners expect a new wife not to have an impact on their kids who are working in the business? The kids will usually resent this new wife, viewing her at best as an interloper but more often as a threat to their inheritance. This may also create significant tension (if not flat-out combat) between the children and their father.

Their concern over their inheritance is well founded. It's their family's business, they've had to make sacrifices to make it a success, and now there's a newcomer who might seduce it away from them. And the kids' fears may be legitimate, especially when the business has been successful (i.e., the owner is affluent) and the new wife is a lot younger. It's amazing how a much younger woman can make a man forget he ever had kids with a prior wife.

Of stepchildren. What about situations where there are multiple sets of children from multiple mothers? How are they supposed to react to all of this? Are the newly arriving stepchildren automatically entitled to positions in the family business? Is this fair to the "original" children? What happens to the children of the ex-wife or -wives?

Of prior wife(s). What if the business becomes more successful after the arrival of a new wife? The prior wife may think that the business is successful because of something she put into place rather than anything the new wife has done, when in reality the new wife provided the spark that ignited the success. If the prior wife still has ownership in the business, will she use this to try to undermine the success or influence of the new wife?

Of the extended business family. Long-term employees often have feelings that are quite similar to those of the owner's kids. They may have been close to the former wife. Will they resent the new wife and try to undermine her business participation, or will she have their full support?

IT'S NOT ALWAYS A CAKEWALK FOR THE NEW WIFE

Unless the new wife is oblivious (and that's possible), she's aware of the potential jealousies, resentment, and obstacles she faces. Let's look at what she's facing: prior wives, kids from previous marriages (both her own and her husband's), other family members (both her own and her husband's), employees, and so on, all of whom may have some problems with her arrival as the new wife. The obstacles are innumerable, and they may come either from the family business or from the family system.

With so much potential mistrust and resentment around her, who else can she turn to for support but her new husband?

THE EX IS GONE—ISN'T SHE?

Sometimes ex-spouses still work in the family businesses. The owners of these businesses seem to believe that it shows how strong or healthy they are that they're able to rise above the divorce and act like true professionals. This is not necessarily the case.

From the workplace. The presence of multiple wives in the business, be they the current and the ex, multiple exes, or some variation thereof, is not healthy for the business system. There is too much baggage if multiple wives are present in the business. When a divorce occurs, one of the spouses—either the husband or the wife—must leave the business, and adding subsequent spouses to the business is a risky proposition. Even if it seems normal to you, it might seem abnormal to your employees, and if they're talented they have the ability to go elsewhere rather than stay and have to deal with the situation.

The reason often given for continuing to employ ex-spouses is that they're "irreplaceable." I've got news for you: few people are truly irreplaceable, especially if you look hard enough for a replacement. The drawbacks of continuing to employ ex-spouses almost universally outweigh any perceived benefits, even from people who were good contributors to the business.

From ownership. What happens if the ex still has an ownership interest in the business? It's important that some type of intervention be used to ensure that the business has that person's cooperation and support. Ex-spouses may try to use their ownership interest to sabotage the business. Even though they're owners, there's no guarantee that they will act in a rational manner to maximize the health of the business.

Divorce

Divorce can bring out the worst in people. It may mean more than the death of a marriage; often it's done in such a way as to guarantee the death of the family business as well.

YOU'LL HATE HER LAWYER MORE THAN YOUR MOTHER-IN-LAW

The key thing to remember is that divorce is not about separating. It's about retribution, payback, and punishment, and the other spouse's attorney has numerous ways of guaranteeing this.

A going-out-of-business sale. Everything must be liquidated on the day of the divorce; if the two spouses can't agree on an equitable settlement, the court will impose one on them. So how do you distribute the family business?

Rather than having to continue to own it, one divorcing spouse can force the other to buy his or her ownership interest in the family business. Where will the money come from? Often the family's only asset is its business, and since the owner doesn't personally have the money to buy the ex out, the only way to raise the money is to sell his or her interest in the business.

Unfortunately, partial ownership of a family business is not a liquid asset. Who'd want it? The only way there's a chance of receiving fair market value for the business is for the entire business to be sold. But then it will no longer be the family's business, and therefore, the former owners will need to find new jobs for themselves elsewhere. The worst-case scenario is when several family members co-own a business—all of their net worth is tied up in that business, and a divorce of one of these owners forces the company to be sold. For example, there was a real estate company owned by two brothers. When one of them divorced, the wife wanted to be paid rather than continue her ownership of the business. Because of the recession in the early 1990s, the business was not generating sufficient profits to pay her, nor were banks lending money. The business had to be dissolved and sold so the one brother could generate the cash needed.

Both Hell and your assets have frozen over. Because of the games many divorcing spouses love to play (e.g., hiding assets, going on spending sprees), courts will often freeze their assets in order to protect the community property prior to determining a distribution. But what happens when the assets are needed to run the business: to purchase supplies, restock inventory, and so on? While the business may be able to obtain credit elsewhere, it will have to do so at a much higher cost, to say nothing of the disruption of normal operations until the divorce is accomplished.

Even the Spanish Inquisition wasn't this detail-oriented. Time equals money, and time spent fighting a divorce is time taken away from running the business. Can the business prosper without your full attention?

If the divorce is ugly, the process of litigation will be lengthy. Attorneys may conduct time-consuming depositions, submit detailed interrogatories, perform valuations, and so forth.

What might have been a quick, simple, and equitable divorce degenerates into an ugly fight over every piece of silverware, and it takes a lot of time.

And that leaves nothing for you. Divorcing spouses seem oblivious to the basic rule of divorce: Whatever happens, the attorneys will be paid.

Conducting an ugly divorce requires that both parties pay a series of fees to their respective experts. There are attorneys' fees, accountants' fees, court reporters' fees, court costs, fees for expert witnesses, fees for private investigators (if they really want to go for the dirt). Where do these fees come from? You've got it: from your assets. And what happens when your only asset is the family business? It will be sold to pay for all of the professional services, leaving both of you without a business, without assets, and, because it's no longer your business, without jobs.

WHAT IS THE COLLATERAL DAMAGE FROM THIS TYPE OF WARFARE?

Any air force officer will tell you that no matter how smart the bomb and how accurate the delivery, there's bound to be some collateral damage. In the same way, ugly divorces have a way of spilling over into the business. They can have bad effects in a number of areas.

On the family. Even though the children may be adults, divorce can amplify the problems of any of them who work in the business. Who are they to side with? How can they stay neutral and continue to perform their jobs? At a minimum, they'll be under considerable stress.

On employees. Because employees in a family business often constitute a kind of extended family, the owner's divorce is in a sense their divorce. The soon-to-be ex-spouse may have been well liked, and the ugliness of the divorce is painful to employees, who will be resentful.

Will employees feel pressured to do things they otherwise wouldn't? For example, husbands love to try to minimize the damage of judgments against them by deflating their income and hiding assets, and may even produce a second set of books and supporting records. Will employees, fearing for their jobs, be pressured to support this charade? Remember, they're usually unemployable elsewhere and won't be able to make the inflated salary they've been paid, and they know it.

On the business. Divorce means that the family system is breaking down and a portion of it being severed. A danger with family businesses is that the family system usually is highly present in the business system and that what happens in the family will spill over into the business. There will be repercussions as family members who are involved in the business system take sides.

Divorce inevitably has an impact on a business's corporate culture. It's hard to quantify or define, but the employees can feel it. There's uncertainty because things will be changing. Also, the business may flounder as family members are distracted by the divorce, and this does not enhance employee morale. Poor morale hampers the business.

In the community. Will the ugliness of the divorce tarnish the business's reputation in the community? Family businesses are often accorded goodwill exactly because customers view the business as an extension of the family. In the event of a divorce—and an ugly one, at that—will people now find it preferable to conduct their business with a different family?

Mistresses and Other Playthings

These situations pose dangers to the business when the relationship is consensual. The emergence of sexual harassment laws also makes these affairs suicidal—you could be putting the family's assets in jeopardy. What today is true love may later become a large judgment when things don't work out.

IT'S NOT AS SECRET AS YOU THINK

I want to let you in on a little secret about what you think is your little secret: everyone knows, especially if the mistress works in the business. Another secret is that a series of dynamics has been set in motion that is undermining the business's health.

Why should I trust you? The fact that someone is the owner's mistress tends to mean, to employees, that they're not trustworthy. By their own actions they're demonstrating that they're willing to step over someone else's needs to grab what they want. Can they blame their coworkers for not trusting them?

Employees are often flat-out afraid of an owner's mistress. By default, the mistress has been given too much power in the organization. It's implicit: if you make the mistress angry, the owner is going to find out. She'll make sure that he does, and somehow you'll be punished.

What else are you not revealing to me? The fact that she's willing to be someone's mistress demonstrates that she's willing to live a life filled with secrets.

Coworkers will inevitably wonder what other key pieces of information are being withheld or filtered. In an effective business, people need access to information. Coworkers are often dependent upon one another for critical information, and it's hard to cooperate with or depend upon someone whose trustworthiness has been compromised.

Wherever she goes, there's the owner. Being a mistress is a sure-fire way of destroying one's professional credibility. A mistress will never be viewed independently; she will always be viewed as a negative extension of the owner. Any good ideas she has or contributions she makes, however good her job performance is, it will always be dismissed as "Oh she's just ———'s mistress."

THE EMPLOYEES YOU NEED DON'T WANT TO DEAL WITH THIS

If you want your business to succeed, you need to fill it with the top talent available. True professionals want to excel: to create new products, to make the next sale, to deliver quality service, to exceed last year's goals. They focus their energies on advancing the business and expect the business to focus its energies likewise.

What top professionals don't want to have to handle is this kind of baggage, and if they're good they'll go elsewhere. Thus, such indiscretions lead to a business staffed with a bunch of marginal performers.

So if you're going to have a mistress, have the decency to find one elsewhere. Let me rephrase that: have the enlightened self-interest to protect your family's business and do it elsewhere.

17

···········

Baggage *du Jour*

The family's baggage presents a series of problems that occur on a random and ongoing basis. It's like the soup in a French restaurant: you know it's going to be good, but you don't know from one day to the next what it is going to be. People working in a family business never know when they're going to be confronted by the following problems, but they do know that the waiter will be rude and the check will be expensive.

They're Stuck

Let's say a partial owner has seen the light and wants to depart the family business to pursue other endeavors. To complete this escape, he or she wants to sell off their ownership interest to fund a new venture. There's just one problem: they can't. Like it or not, that person is stuck in the family business.

A RESTRICTIVE COVENANT THAT'S LEGAL

Owners are often contractually prohibited from selling their ownership in the family business to "outsiders." Perhaps an owner can sell it only to family members who already own an interest, or only to blood relatives, or only to their children. Consequently, ownership may be purchased only by a limited number of buyers.

Owners are trapped unless they can force the other owners to buy them out. Without this safety valve, an owner's livelihood, assets, and possibly even nest egg is unjustly locked into the family's business.

WE'D LIKE TO HELP, BUT WE DON'T HAVE ANY MONEY

Let's say the owner has a wonderful family and everyone supports his or her desire to leave. There's still another obstacle to overcome: Do they have the money for a buyout?

Let's think about this for a moment. If the family business is small, where do you suppose everyone's money is? You've got it; it's probably locked up in the business. Even though they may want to purchase the ownership interest, they simply do not have the money.

Let's get it from the bank. One source of funds might be a loan from a bank. Banks traditionally make loans to enable businesses to take actions that strengthen and grow the business (e.g., providing capital for expansion, for new equipment, for inventory). But where's the increased strength or improvement in simply reallocating ownership? Would a bank make a loan for this purpose?

Who pays? Even if a bank authorizes a loan, there are other sources of potential conflict: Who will pay the interest? Is it fair to make the buyers pay the cost of the interest on the loan? On the other hand, is it fair for the departing owner to have to absorb the cost of the interest?

Can't we use the profits? The business may get creative and try to fund an owner's buyout by using its future profits. This raises several issues. First, what guarantee is there that the business will have sufficient profits to pay for the purchase? It may be many years before the business yields enough cash. Second, should selling owners still have a voice in the company while they're receiving installments? After all, they haven't received all their money, so they should still have some say in matters. Then again, they wanted to leave and the remaining owners have bought them out.

WOULD YOU BUY USED BAGGAGE FROM THIS MAN?

Even if ownership can be sold outside the family, problems remain.

Why would an outsider want to buy into this mess? When an outside buyer acquires ownership interest in a family business, that buyer also acquires the family baggage. The new owner will always be an outsider forced to deal with co-owners who are tied together by relationship and by a history probably unknown to him or her.

Where's the economic benefit? The only reason to buy a piece of a business is the expectation of making money from it. If a buyer is buying a minority interest in the business, he or she probably believes that payment will take the form of dividends or a share of the profits. But how can this be guaranteed based on only a minority interest?

If becoming an owner means that the buyer will have a job in the business, is there any guarantee that he or she will get along with the other owners and family members? It's a pretty risky commitment just to get a job.

WHAT'S IT WORTH?

A lot of accountants and financial advisors specialize in valuing businesses. These seem like the logical people to use when trying to determine the fair value of an ownership interest in a family business. Unfortunately, while these people are very competent to take a quantitative approach in valuation, they miss critical qualitative aspects (i.e., the family baggage) that have a significant impact on the business's value. The presence of family baggage in a family business requires a discount in the price. However the assets may appear on paper or to the unknowing eye, they are not worth as much as they may seem.

HOW MANY PIECES OF SILVER DID YOU GET FOR THIS BETRAYAL?

We live in an era of continual mergers, acquisitions, and consolidations, and many family businesses are attractive to other companies. While there may be opportunities to sell the business, many owners are prevented from doing so.

You're the reason it's no longer the family's business. If a majority interest in a family business is sold to an outsider, the family business has effectively been killed. It's no longer owned by the family; it's owned by someone else.

Anytime someone acquires controlling interest in a company, it's only logical to assume that they're going to want to take over and clean out the deadwood, be they family members or long-tenured employees.

The family will remember what you did . . . Whoever sold the controlling interest will be blamed if family members and long-tenured employees are downsized. The price of creating trauma, inflicting economic hardship on family members, and betraying the family's informal promise to continue to employ loyal long-term employees is excommunication. As a practical matter, I wouldn't expect to be invited over for Thanksgiving.

. . . even if nothing bad happens. Even if none of the Doomsday scenarios outlined above occurs, there's always the probability that some of the family will never understand. These people's identity is enmeshed in being a part of their family's business, and the sale threatens them. It doesn't matter that outwardly nothing has happened—there have been no layoffs or policy changes—or if they might have profited from the sale (i.e., the business is healthier, they have been given offers to sell their interests at an increased price); inwardly they valued working for what they always perceived was their family's business.

Problems Resulting from Who Owns What

Spreading the ownership of a family business among different family members can create a series of conflicts. The most obvious involves how the pie was sliced: Did everyone get the same-size serving?

But another set of issues arises from the nature of each person's ownership and his or her participation in the business. This is a more subtle source of conflict, yet the problems it produces are just as potent as those arising when people feel they didn't get a fair slice.

BEST INTERESTS VERSUS PERCEIVED BEST INTERESTS

Conflict arises when different owners actively pursue what they believe is in their own best interest, because each owner has potentially differing (and conflicting) economic interests. The three primary contestants doing battle are as follows: the business, owners who work in the business, and owners who do not work in the business.

The best interests of the business. A business does not remain viable on its own. For a business to remain viable, continual investment in itself is required, be it in the form of capital investments such as new equipment or hardware or in the form of training and development to strengthen the skills of its employees.

The primary source of money for investing in a family business is often the business's profits. The only problem with this is that profits earmarked for reinvestment would otherwise be available to be paid out as dividends; thus, keeping the business viable requires diverting profits away from dividends. Some owners do not like this.

The best interests of owners working in the family business. Owners who are employed by the business find that their best interests are tied to those of the business itself. In other words, the best way to protect their jobs and salaries is to keep the business as healthy as possible.

The perceived best interests of owners who do not work in the family business. Owners who do not work in the family business do not receive a salary (at least they're not supposed to). The only way these owners receive an economic benefit from the business is through the payout of dividends. Therefore, their perceived best interest is to insist that the business continually pay dividends.

But what happens when the business desperately needs reinvestment to keep it viable? Common sense would dictate that these owners' best interest is to align themselves with the best interests of the business itself, but common sense does not always prevail. They've usually grown accustomed to receiving their dividends, so there's a temptation to undermine the viability of the business by demanding the payment of dividends regardless of business necessities.

Even in situations where common sense is applied, it is often difficult for people not working in the business to fully appreciate the conditions in the business. It is easy for well-intentioned owners not to realize the extent of reinvestment needed and to mistakenly insist on dividends.

STICK YOUR NOSE SOMEPLACE ELSE

The existence of multiple owners, some who do and others who do not work in the business, can create resentment and tension.

Someone's getting a free ride. Owners who work in the business often work hard to keep it going. But what happens when they see that their co-owners aren't working with them to keep the business going? It's natural for working owners to believe that absentee owners enjoy the benefits of owning a business without having to earn a living.

In reality, owners who do not work in the family business are usually fully employed elsewhere. They have to earn a living just like the family members who are working for the family business. Unfortunately, working owners don't witness the absentee owners' labor.

"What do you know? You don't have all the facts!" While they may not work in the family business, absentee owners do have a legitimate interest in what's happening. Unfortunately,

working owners may be overly sensitive to any questions or inquiries posed by absentee owners. What are often legitimate questions or inquiries tend to be interpreted as unwarranted intrusions.

PUT CONTROL INTO THE HANDS OF THE OWNERS WHO NEED IT

One way to help minimize the inherent conflict between working owners and absentee owners is to place control of the business in the proper hands.

Owners working in the business need control . . . The owners who are actively working in the family business and who are in senior management positions are the ones who should have the voting or controlling ownership interest. Effectively run businesses require people who have the authority to make and implement decisions and the ability to do so in a timely manner. Because the best interests of employed owners are aligned with the best interests of the business, giving those owners controlling authority tends to increase the likelihood that they will take actions consistent with keeping the business viable.

But, just because the best interests of owners working in the business are aligned with those of the business itself, there is no guarantee that these owners will actually make the proper decisions. Something more is needed.

. . . but also require a "check" to safeguard the interests of other owners. There is a danger that the owners working in the business will be so caught up in day-to-day problems that they will lose sight of key strategic issues.

As a safeguard, family businesses should utilize the services of a Council of Advisors or other outside advisors. Their function is to help oversee the strategic issues affecting the business. In other words, the managing owners are free to make the day-to-day operating decisions unfettered by unneeded—and unwanted—interference from absentee owners, while the use of outside advisors helps protect the long-term interests of all owners.

"Change" Is a Dirty Word

Most family systems are quite resistant to change. It's therefore no surprise that the businesses owned by these families are also resistant to change.

THE TIMES THEY ARE A-CHANGING

All businesses, be they small family businesses or *Fortune* 500 corporations, operate in a marketplace that is continually changing. If anything, the speed and impact of change have been accelerating significantly over the past several decades, and the pace can only be expected to continue to increase. This means that in order to remain viable, family businesses have to be able to make changes to remain in touch with the marketplace.

Unfortunately, family businesses often want to stick their head in the sand and insist that there's no need to change. A danger with sticking one's head in the sand is that it makes it a lot easier for predators to come along and bite you in the rump.

THE OWNERS ARE BUSY ACTING LIKE PARENTS

Family-business owners often treat their employees as though they were extended members of the family. As such, the employees are discouraged from actively participating in business decisions or problem solving.

This raises obstacles to change. First, any change will have to be initiated and imposed by the owners. Second, the owners might be too busy handling day-to-day problems to recognize or understand the changes that need to be made. Third, even if the owners do understand the need for change, there is no assurance that they have the proper skills to effect it. Finally, if the employees have learned to act like dependent children, there's nothing to indicate that they possess the drive, self-initiative, or skills to implement the changes that are being asked of them.

THOSE DREADED LONG-TENURED EMPLOYEES (AGAIN)

Family businesses tend to have employees who have been working there a long time. These employees usually have a strong desire to maintain the status quo, which runs smack in the face of a business needing to make changes. They have become comfortable with the current surroundings and situation and thus will naturally resist any changes. It's a combination of comfort with the status quo, fear of the unknown, and inability to conquer the unknown.

A STRONG SENSE OF TRADITION

Family businesses tend to have a strong sense of tradition. Businesses with a strong sense of tradition tend to have corporate cultures that are resistant to change, unless a key tenet within their corporate culture is to value change. A corporate culture that values change is rare, and a family tradition that

speaks of the importance of valuing change is even rarer; therefore, it's safe to conclude that it's hard to find a family business
with a corporate culture that embraces and encourages change.

Instead, the corporate cultures of most family businesses act
as self-reenforcing mechanisms that resist change. Family
members put strong pressure on one another to continue any
traditions that are a part of the business.

WE OVERCAME LONG ODDS TO BE SUCCESSFUL

The reality is that most start-up businesses fail—and rather
quickly. Businesses that are able to hang on for several years
are often a testament more to the presence of a substantial nest
egg that is backing up the business than to the business owner's
acumen.

A family business that has been around more than a decade
has overcome long odds. Having beaten these long odds can
breed an unfortunate belief within these businesses that any
challenges can be overcome. The danger in such situations is
that the owners feel that there is no need to worry about change
because their business has always overcome obstacles. These
owners fail to see the dangers inherent in a rapidly changing
marketplace.

"What Price Success?" on the Kids

The people who start family businesses—namely, the
parents—tend to think that they're the ones who make all the
sacrifices involved in starting and building the business. That's
not true. The children usually pay a price, though it is seldom
recognized or understood.

HOW OLD WERE THE CHILDREN WHEN THE BUSINESS BECAME SUCCESSFUL?

There is a strong correlation between the age of the children, the arrival of the business's success, and the children's ambition and assumptions.

The predicaments of being older when success arrived. Children who were older when the business became successful often saw their parents work long and hard to build the business. In many cases, these children also worked in the business, helping to contribute to its success. As a result, they either develop a good work ethic or are deeply resentful of the sacrifices they had to make. Either way, they realize how difficult building a business can be because they experienced firsthand the sacrifices needed to build one. These children also remember that the business has not always been successful; they don't automatically assume that the business will survive indefinitely.

The predicaments of being younger when success arrived. Children who were young when the business became successful tend to have a different outlook from those who were older. These children have experienced only a business that is successful, and as a result they often fail to understand the sacrifices that were made to make it a success. They may dangerously assume that success is easy to achieve or that the business will automatically continue to be successful. Who can blame them? After all, their only experience with the family's business has been that it is a success.

These younger children are often able to escape the sacrifices made by their older brothers and sisters because the business is finally successful, the money is flowing in, and it's natural for the parents to want to enjoy the fruits of their labor. Unfortunately, they may spread these fruits a little too generously upon children who haven't developed the character to appreciate it. Parents have a tendency to overindulge or spoil these children, and lots of people are made miserable because of this.

MOM ALWAYS LIKED *YOU* BEST

If there is a big spread in the children's ages, the stage is set for potential strife. In most families, the older children experienced the struggle to build the business, working hard at menial tasks. Their younger brothers and sisters got a free ride because they were either too young or the business was already successful and their help wasn't needed. In spite of the different sacrifices made, the parents may eventually reward all of the children equally, and then the conflict starts. Or the older children may be given greater rewards for their sacrifices, their younger brothers and sisters don't understand why, and then the conflict starts.

One of the worst situations I've seen was a family where the two oldest brothers worked part-time in the family's struggling construction business throughout high school and full-time while going to college. The business then became very successful. Their younger brother never worked there. In fact, he wasn't required to work summer jobs during high school or college because the family now had plenty of money. Unfortunately, the parents gave all three brothers equal ownership in the business, and the two brothers haven't spoken to their younger brother in more than a decade.

The issue of whether the children had significantly different experiences while growing up is one that families need to address, even if it seems as if it isn't an issue. There are three possibilities: it may truly be a nonissue (that's unlikely); it may seem like a nonissue (the children have mastered the art of repressing their anger); or the family may successfully lance a festering wound that would have continued to grow worse (it was an issue after all).

Then again, maybe Tom Smothers understood such a family's baggage: "Mom always liked *you* best."

18

....

The American Dream Versus the Family Nightmare

A force is emerging in the U.S. economy that will grow increasingly more powerful in the next few decades: the family-owned businesses of immigrants. These businesses succeed where others fail because the entire family is committed to the business's success.

The Road to Emigrate Is Fraught with Peril

Numerous challenges confront people who immigrate to the United States. Some of these challenges are faced by all family members, while others are peculiar to individuals.

CLASHING CULTURES AND THE PRESSURES TO CONFORM

Emigrating to a new country means that people physically leave one culture and enter a new one. The reality is that immigrants never fully leave their old culture.

Immigrants may be caught in a no-win situation: they face

pressure to conform to dual cultures—the old and the new—yet they feel that embracing one culture means betraying the other. The differences between the cultures and the pressures to conform (from both cultures) are sources of conflict.

The Old World equates with rigidity. People who immigrate to the United States tend to come from countries with cultures that are older and that value tradition. These cultures have clearly defined expectations regarding roles within the family. They are often male-dominated and insist on respect for one's elders. A family unit usually includes extended family, and there are deeply held expectations that the young will take care of their elders.

The United States is an open society. In contrast to the Old World, the United States is a flexible society without rigidly imposed boundaries. Despite what the upsurge of neoconservative and fundamentalist rhetoric would have you believe, we've advanced technologically and economically specifically by rejecting the rigid traditions and superstitions of the Old World.

DILEMMAS FACING THE PARENTS

The process of immigrating carries a series of challenges that can hamper one's ability to run a family business.

Finding one's way in a strange land. There are innumerable differences between an immigrant's native country and the United States, and the process of figuring out how things are done can be daunting. What are the local customs and practices? What hours are the banks open? How do I . . . ?

The most basic obstacle to navigating in this new society is the inability to speak English, which is often not the immigrant's native language.

Earning a living. Starting a family business is a daunting task. Immigrants must do everything anyone else would do to start a business, but they must figure out how to do this within the context of a foreign system. The way one would have started a business back home may be entirely different from how it's done here.

Raising kids. Raising children is a full-time job without all the additional time demands and obstacles resulting from being an immigrant. While all parents share universal worries about the well-being of their children, immigrants have an additional fear: What new, different, undesirable traits will their children pick up in this new country?

Keeping in touch. Even though they decided to emigrate, immigrants may have strong connections with family and friends in their former country. Maintaining contact with them often creates a dilemma: To what extent will family members in the old country expect the émigrés to continue to conform to the traditions and cultures of the old country and their family?

Sometimes the slightest change can bring immediate condemnation: "You've become Americanized." Embracing aspects of the new culture is viewed as betraying one's ancestors.

DILEMMAS FACING THE KIDS

Children in immigrant families face the dilemma of trying to conform to conflicting systems, cultures, and expectations.

They can conform to their parents' system and endure the taunts and ostracism of their peers, they can fully assimilate and fight an intergenerational conflict with their family, or they can try to develop chameleon-type skills.

Strangers in their own homes. Their home is either a bastion of their parent's country, culture, and traditions (and often language) or a bizarre hodgepodge of their parents' native country and the United States. Unlike their American friends, who merely have to master the quirkiness of their parents at home, these kids must learn how to master two differing systems. While they're at home, there's one system, and their family tells them that it's normal. Yet they're continually bombarded with conflicting messages when they go to school or over to their friends' house to play. Some children move easily between these differing worlds. For others, it's not so easy.

Presented with these conflicting systems, they may never feel completely at home in their new country because they fail to assimilate fully. Yet if they become too Americanized, they may never feel completely at home even in their own home.

Strangers in their homeland. Even if the children were born abroad, they were often too young to remember much about their native country. There's no reason for them to have an affinity with their homeland since they often remember nothing of it other than what their family has told them. Often they pretend to have an affiliation with that country, simply to please their family.

The Americanization process. The process of the children becoming Americanized may be a source of considerable conflict within an immigrant-owned business. The trauma is big enough if the family came from a culture that stresses obedience to elders and the Americanized children are asserting themselves against the elder generation, but the kids may also try to interject all of the crazy ideas they've learned in their new country into the family's business.

Immigrants come to the United States to pursue a better life. But part of that better life is that the children will inevitably become Americanized. You can't pick and choose which parts of the dream you'll get. For example, if I fall in love with a Frenchwoman and emigrate to Paris to build our life together, I have no right to complain if our children develop a taste for old Jerry Lewis movies.

THE FAMILY MAY HAVE TRAVELED FAR TO IMMIGRATE, BUT THERE'S NO DISTANCE BETWEEN ITS MEMBERS

When it first arrived, the family had to pull together to learn how to navigate in the new country. But as its members transition, they should start to give one another distance as the reason for their pulling together gradually dissipates.

Remember, firecrackers were introduced from distant lands. There are probably tremendous unresolved issues among the family members in immigrant-owned businesses. It's a veritable powder keg ready to explode.

The reason the conflict is not resolved is because it's so strongly repressed by the burden of family obligations. But a business cannot achieve its full potential when its employees' efforts are based on fulfilling a sense of obligation. Employees need to have passion for their work; otherwise they simply go through the motions.

The business might succeed, might endure, at the price of family members never achieving their full potential elsewhere (if allowed to flee the family's business) or making their maximum contribution to the family's business (had they been allowed the distance to resolve family issues).

Who needs Berlitz when we've got the kids? Problems arise if the parents don't assimilate—more precisely, if they don't learn to speak English. The children can't distance themselves from the family because they're forced into a form of indentured servitude. It's a reverse variation of making older kids take their younger brothers and sisters along when they go out to play. The blunt reality is this: except when they are within their expatriate community, non-English-speaking parents need a translator to interact in society. The most convenient source of translation services is the kids.

The children may initially be dragged into the family business as translators. They're efficient, and the price is right. Unfortunately, there may be pressure for them to continue working in the business, especially if the parents don't assimilate. If the parents' culture stresses obeying family elders and adhering to family-defined roles, they will expect their children to continue to work in the business, and their continuing employment will create the potential for conflict.

All aboard! If the family's culture defines "family" as the extended family, there is often strong pressure to re-create this extended family in the business. The owners of the business are expected and obligated to find a job for their entire extended family. Anyone who can make it to the United States is automatically included; their qualifications to work in the business are irrelevant.

In some cultures, the notion of extended family is so strong that an emigrating member is obligated to sponsor any and all relatives who want to emigrate. Sponsorship includes providing a source of livelihood—in the family business. It's hard for the family to transition and assimilate into the U.S. culture when a continual infusion of fresh blood reinforces the old ways.

Struggling to Find the Best Way to Do Things

A series of issues arises from the differences between the United States and the person's native country, and trying to determine the best solutions can be challenging.

CLASHING CULTURES IN THE WORKPLACE

For several years, the issue of increasing diversity in the workplace (and society as well) has been the subject of many articles in both the business and academic literature. The thesis of the literature is that the people entering the U.S. workforce are no longer predominantly white and male and that, to be effective, businesses will have to find ways of managing people with diverse backgrounds.

But what happens when it is the owners themselves who are injecting the different culture into the workplace? This is exactly what happens in an immigrant-owned situation. By default, the owners impose their own culture on the management and workers. Several issues revolve around whether the culture of the immigrant-owned business is in sync with the culture of its workers or that of the marketplace (i.e., its customers).

The culture and values of the owners (and their family). Their name is on the door. Therefore, whatever culture the immigrant owners bring with them is the one that will ultimately prevail.

In an immigrant business, the culture of the owning family is critical. It must be understood in great detail because it will have an impact upon how the business is run. The values and beliefs of the owners serve as a lens through which they view their business. It will help determine how they go about running their business: the products and services offered, the management practices used, the type of customer service delivered.

The culture and values of the employees. To what extent do the culture and values of the employees differ from those of the immigrant owners? What disagreements or conflicts will these differences create?

The difficulty in answering these questions stems from the fact that the U.S. workforce is itself diverse. Rather than the employees sharing a single culture, there may be several cultures present. If this is the case, no single approach or solution can be readily applied. The owners need to find a way to interact with their employees' diverse cultures. The danger is that it may be possible to make one segment of employees happy while unintentionally antagonizing others.

Getting maximum performance from employees requires that immigrant owners show sensitivity to their culture(s). But will the owners' culture allow them to do this?

The culture and values of the customers. Customers also have their own culture and values, which may be different from those of both the owners and the employees. Just as with the employees, the customers themselves may not have a single culture. The worst-case scenario is when immigrant owners manage employees from several cultures in a business serving customers from a different set of cultures.

Ultimately, in order to maximize its sales and be successful, the business must conform to the customers' culture(s). Again, will the immigrant owners' culture allow them to do this?

DOES THE CULTURE OF THE OLD COUNTRY INHIBIT THE ADOPTION OF EFFECTIVE BUSINESS PRACTICES?

The corporate culture of a business controls how that business operates. In immigrant situations, the family's culture—the one they bring with them from their homeland—is the controlling corporate culture.

This possibility—that the culture is inhibiting effective business practices—should always be a red flag to any competent business advisor.

For example, in my business travels in the Middle East I have encountered Afghan merchants who would not sell me their entire supply of wares. The reason given was that if they sold everything to me they wouldn't be able to stand there for the rest of the day and sell their wares to anyone else. (No, rationing was not in effect.) The notion of replenishing their supply and generating further sales that same day was beyond their comprehension—it was a foreign concept.

Coming from countries with less enlightened labor laws. The United States has long been industrialized. We also have a long history of a labor movement fighting to improve the conditions of workers and a standard of living that is sufficiently high to give us the luxury of doing so. This is not to say that things here are perfect. In the early years of our industrialization there were some horrible working conditions, and even today there are the working poor, who are trapped in minimum-wage jobs. The important thing, however, is that we have a sense of how things ought to be.

If immigrant owners come from the Third World, they are

coming from countries that have only recently industrialized, that tend to have less developed traditions of a labor movement, and whose economies simply cannot afford the luxury of providing workers with high wages or decent working conditions. In addition, they may be coming from cultures that have a very traditional master-servant orientation in the workplace.

"May I help you? . . . Have a nice day!" Part of United States business culture is a sense of customer service and courtesy. This has become increasingly important over the past decade as the United States has seen significant growth in the service sector of the economy. However, is the notion of customer service and courtesy a part of the immigrant business culture? To the extent it is not, immigrant-owned businesses are placing themselves at a distinct disadvantage.

A possible obstacle to a customer service or courtesy orientation is linguistic or cross-cultural miscommunication. Is there something in the tone, cadence, delivery, mannerisms, or body language of immigrants that may be misinterpreted by their customers?

This question is not as far-fetched as it might seem. For example, in the wake of the 1992 Los Angeles riots (or uprising, as some cultures would define it), there was a movement in the Korean community to conduct courses in customer service practices for Korean business owners in the belief that some of their mannerisms had led to these businesses becoming alienated from community residents, who subsequently targeted them for looting.

Other Obstacles and Booby-Traps

There is a series of additional unique issues that immigrant-owned businesses must deal with if they are to maximize their success.

YOU MAY SPEAK THE LANGUAGE, BUT DO YOU UNDERSTAND WHAT'S BEING SAID?

In the United States, the self-help sections of bookstores are filled with books on relationships stating that the reason men and women don't get along is that we use the same words but attach different meanings to them. If people from the same culture attach different meanings to the same words, what's to prevent this from happening with people coming from foreign cultures whose native language isn't English?

How do you know what Americans want? The only way for any business to survive is for it to deliver what the marketplace wants. But how can business owners know what the marketplace wants—the tastes, desires, and preferences of customers—if they're not from here? Immigrant-owned businesses are at a disadvantage to the extent that their owners are not fully in sync with the American culture and marketplace.

One potential solution to this dilemma is for immigrant-owned businesses to deliver basic commodity products or services (e.g., taxi service, convenience minimarts, electronics stores, fast-food outlets). These types of businesses represent a safe option because basic needs tend to transcend cultural preferences in the marketplace.

But what if an immigrant-owned business wants to offer products or services over and above these basic needs?

Immigrant owners must learn to look beyond their natural cultural biases and instead try to determine what it is that the overall market wants. They don't need to learn formal market research techniques; it can merely be an innate sense of what people want.

Is serving your own community too narrow a niche? One effective way to avoid having to learn what Americans want is for an immigrant-owned business to restrict its activities to serving the members of its own expatriate community. If there is a large, tightly knit community, such a strategy avoids many of the problems associated with assimilation.

While this may seem like a safe strategy, it is important to examine its viability in the long run. Is it possible that the older generation of the expatriate community is dying off and their children have become assimilated and are moving out of the neighborhood and going elsewhere? If so, the immigrant-owned business has locked itself into a dwindling market.

As a general rule, it's safest for immigrant-owned businesses to learn how to serve the market at large. Reaching beyond the confines of one's own expatriate community offers the potential for limitless expansion.

FINDING A QUALIFIED ADVISOR

All businesses need advisors, such as accountants, attorneys, and consultants. Immigrant-owned businesses can benefit from these advisors because the right advisor(s) can expedite the business's learning curve and help it to avoid mistakes it would otherwise make.

Do American advisors understand the cross-cultural issues? Immigrant organizations have a unique set of problems revolving around cross-cultural issues. Correctly addressing these issues is critical, and immigrant owners must screen their advisors to ensure that they have the ability to understand these cross-cultural issues. Otherwise, they will get advice that is technically correct yet totally worthless because it's not implementable.

How Americanized are the advisors in your ethnic community? It's natural for immigrant business owners to want to use advisors within their own expatriate community. They speak the language and understand the culture and values. But there's a problem with doing so; immigrant business owners are not in their homeland. They're in a new country, and they need to adapt to the new environment.

To receive worthwhile advice, business owners must employ advisors who fully understand the marketplace of the new country. In other words, they must be Americanized. Otherwise, they will look out into the marketplace through the same biased lens that the immigrant business owners do. For example, if I have a legal problem, I talk to a top attorney rather than to someone like myself who has merely attended law school. If immigrant owners need an attorney, do they go to someone who might not have a full command of English? Our legal system is based on the effective use of English, and such an attorney would make an ineffective advocate.

Will you listen to an Americanized advisor? For an immigrant-owned business to be successful, it must apply the business practices that are most effective here in the United States. The people who are best qualified to give this advice come from one of two groups: within the immigrant community, they are Americanized persons who are able to reach forward into the culture of the new homeland; or they are the rare Americans who are able to reach back to the native culture to understand the cross-cultural issues facing immigrants.

Predators in their own community. A danger with being a stranger in a strange land is the need to trust advisor(s) when confronted with unfamiliar situations. The increase in immigrant-owned businesses has seen an accompanying increase in a disturbing trend: criminals who deliberately target the vulnerabilities of newly arrived immigrants in their own ethnic communities.

A recent *Los Angeles Times* article said that local police authorities have set up special task forces to counter this type of crime. What they have found is that recently arrived immigrants tend to be more trusting of the members of their own expatriate community. Being unfamiliar with U.S. practices yet trusting of their own ethnic advisors makes them too accepting and too easily swindled.

Parting Advice

Immigrant owners can take two actions to increase the chances of their business's success.

ASSIMILATE

Immigrants should retain the best aspects of what they brought from their homeland. These are assets that must be preserved and treasured.

But being effective in a new homeland requires assimilation. Time must be taken to learn a new culture and to apply new practices to day-to-day living. This is especially true with regard to business. In addition, English must be mastered; otherwise the inability to speak English will act as a barrier to full participation in the society.

Like it or not, the children will eventually assimilate; the danger with the immigrants themselves not assimilating is that they will eventually become an unfair burden that future generations will have to carry.

ACCEPT THE FACT THAT THE CHILDREN MUST GO THEIR OWN WAY—AND LET GO

If the immigrants' culture includes a sense of obligation on the part of the younger generation, this notion must be discarded. The children should not be pressured to go into or carry on the family business. Instead, they should be encouraged to discover what it is they enjoy most and to make their livelihoods pursuing that. Otherwise, the stage is set for pointless conflict within the family, and this will spill over into the family business, hindering its profitability.

The immigrant is the one that brought the family to this new land of opportunity, so he or she should insist that the children take advantage of the new opportunities available. This is the land of freedom, and that freedom is supposed to extend to family members.

PART V

All Is Not Lost

Recommendations and Solutions

You'll notice that the recommendations and solutions presented in this book are not quick fixes. Rather, they require serious work on the part of family businesses. If properly pursued, they will create a long-term advantage for a family business.

Compare what your business is doing against these recommendations. Are you implementing them? What benefits have you seen from doing so? What problems have been eliminated? What setbacks avoided? If you haven't implemented these recommendations: Why not? Can you afford not to?

19

....

Create a Council of Advisors

Family businesses cannot maximize their success without the help of outside advisors. But simply hiring advisors is not the solution; the key is to find the right ones.

The Traditional Lose-Lose Dilemma
When Seeking Advice

Family-business owners have been unable to find people who could solve their problems because traditionally there has not been any group of advisors who possessed the correct mix of expertise and skills. There were people who either knew something about business (but even this was too specialized) and nothing about the root cause of their problems, or people who understood family baggage and knew nothing about business. No wonder things seldom got fixed.

TWO SEPARATE AREAS OF EXPERTISE THAT ARE
TOTALLY WORTHLESS UNLESS INTEGRATED WITH
EACH OTHER

The two types of experts generally used by family businesses are accountants and psychologists. Each, however, brings to the table only half the expertise needed to deal with the problems of the typical family business. This problem is illustrated in Figure 7.

FIGURE 7

The Traditional Lose-Lose Dilemma When Seeking Advice

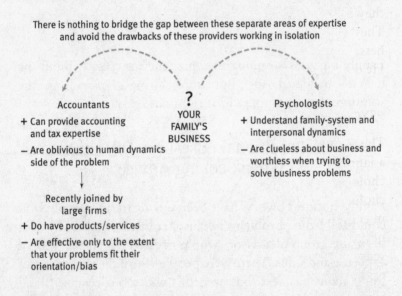

There is nothing to bridge the gap between these separate areas of expertise and avoid the drawbacks of these providers working in isolation

?
YOUR
FAMILY'S
BUSINESS

Accountants

+ Can provide accounting and tax expertise

− Are oblivious to human dynamics side of the problem

Recently joined by large firms

+ Do have products/services

− Are effective only to the extent that your problems fit their orientation/bias

Psychologists

+ Understand family-system and interpersonal dynamics

− Are clueless about business and worthless when trying to solve business problems

WHAT DO ACCOUNTANTS KNOW ABOUT FAMILY BAGGAGE?

The advisors family businesses rely on the most are their accountants. That's fine as long as the problem involves either accounting or tax matters, but this is frightening when you realize that the problems that are killing family businesses have absolutely nothing to do with accounting or tax issues.

It's the family baggage that's killing family businesses, and how can you possibly expect accountants to understand family-system dynamics? About the best they can do is try to determine some kind of book value for the baggage. If they're really creative, they'll even come up with a depreciation schedule for it. For example, a partner at a large accounting firm was exasperated. He was doing succession planning, but his client was insisting on actions that didn't minimize taxes: "What's wrong with them? I keep showing them my calculations, and they don't care about saving an additional ten million dollars. They tell me it doesn't meet their needs." "It's a family business," I said, "and succession has nothing to do with money." He didn't understand what I was saying.

PSYCHOBABBLE DOESN'T HELP EITHER

The people who are best able to understand the root cause of a family business's problems—the family baggage—are psychologists and psychiatrists. But there's a problem with psychologists—a big one: they are totally clueless about business in general and therefore worthless when trying to solve business problems. They might come up with solutions that make sense at home but are totally impractical in the business. For example, one winery enlisted a psychologist to deal with the children's conflict. The psychologist correctly understood that underlying feelings of jealousy were causing the children to fight and that treating all the children equally would promote harmony. Unfortunately, in order to promote this harmony, the psychologist recommended that all the children be given equal ownership and that they share the job of president by having rotating six-month terms.

Finally, bear in mind this essential question: If you need family therapy, why the hell are you all in business together?

IT'S TIME TO BRIDGE THE GAP

There is an alternative to the lose-lose scenario of having to choose between someone who can help families with a narrow segment of their business's problems (i.e., tax and accounting matters) or someone who can help them with family interactions. This alternative can bridge both of the disparate areas of expertise—the business and family systems—and then take it to the next level. This alternative is a Council of Advisors.

The Council of Advisors

OVERVIEW

The function of a Council of Advisors is illustrated in Figure 8. Note that the advisors' areas of expertise, not the experts themselves, are highlighted.

As noted in Figure 8, a family business needs seasoned, well-rounded business expertise, not specialized accounting expertise. In addition, the business needs the understanding of family systems to identify the family's baggage problems.

The triad of advisors who should be full-time members of this council are a consultant, a business lawyer, and an accountant. These three types of advisors together bring the expertise necessary for solving family-business problems.

You want to keep it somewhat informal. A Council of Advisors is not intended to be a formal board of directors. The key to this council is that it consists of advisors, not people who control the business.

One of the advantages of an informal council is that it is relatively unintimidating to family members. They need to feel

FIGURE 8

Providing Your Buisness with the Expertise It Needs

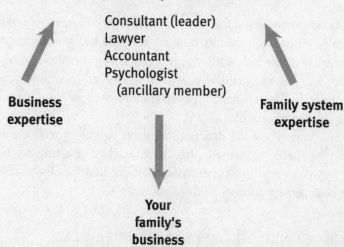

Council of Advisors

Integrates and applies the expertise relevant
to your family's business

Consultant (leader)
Lawyer
Accountant
Psychologist
(ancillary member)

**Business
expertise**

**Family system
expertise**

**Your
family's
business**

comfortable with their advisors, and this informality helps them to open up and reveal what they're really thinking and doing. This honesty from family members and others in the business provides the advisors with crucial information.

Regular meetings. The Council of Advisors should periodically meet with the owner and other key managers of the business, perhaps every three months, or more frequently if needed. The purpose of these meetings is to review the business's progress and to see if people are accomplishing the goals that have been set for them. In addition, these meetings often provide a forum for problem solving should any new problems or issues arise.

Ad hoc meetings. The most common interactions between the family business and council members should be a series of ad hoc meetings, usually one on one with individual council members.

Instead of waiting for a full council meeting, members of the family's business should contact the advisor whose area of expertise is needed. Rather than have family members struggle with a problem until the next formal council meeting occurs, these ad hoc meetings help keep the business moving by solving problems quickly.

It is important for council members to keep their comembers properly informed after each ad hoc meeting to help ensure that they don't give advice that unintentionally conflicts or counteracts another council member's.

THE COUNCIL MEMBERS AND THEIR ROLES

Each council member has a reason for being on the council and a corresponding role. The family business benefits when members adhere to these roles.

Consultant—the ringleader. Consultants should be the primary advisors, and as such they should lead the council. The best way to view consultants is to say that they are analogous to the lead surgeon on a trauma team. They can't do it on their own—they need the services of everyone in the emergency room to do their work—but they are the ones who see the complete situation, set the direction, and coordinate the efforts of sometimes several surgeons operating on different parts of the patient.

In addition to providing the primary business advice to the family business, consultants also coordinate the use of specialists. When a specialized technical problem is identified, they will recognize it and call for a person who has the necessary expertise. Consultants will then work with the specialists to help define the scope of the project and should oversee their work to ensure that it is in alignment with where the business is headed.

Lawyer—advisor and street fighter. It is absolutely essential that the attorneys hired understand business. They should specialize as business attorneys and preferably have a business degree (undergraduate). Although consultants are the lead advisors, lawyers supplement their advice. Attorneys also help act as a counterbalance to accountants' tendency to focus on numbers.

Lawyers need to have the right psychological orientation. They should not be afraid of street fighting. Unfortunately, many business lawyers have a timid disposition and project this onto their clients. As a result, the advice they offer is too cautious. Good lawyers will do two things: they will stay out of fights that don't need to be fought, and they will not be afraid of fighting if they know their position is correct and justified.

Accountant—the "silent" partner. Even though accountants are full and equal members of the council, they need to understand that they are not in the lead role. Their role is much like that of an anesthesiologist, who is there to support the lead surgeon, not to dictate the course of treatment. It's true that an operation can't be performed without an anesthesiologist, but someone else needs to be in charge. Many accountants do not like or accept this role. Unfortunately, their belief that numbers are infallible is sometimes so strong that they take on the zeal of a missionary trying to convert people. Their role must be clearly articulated from the beginning to prevent any misunderstandings.

Accountants need to understand finance as well as accounting. What's the difference? Finance tends to have a more forward-looking perspective, as opposed to accounting, which is often after-the-fact scorekeeping. Finance has a more strategic orientation, and accountants who are also competent financially can help show the dollar implications of differing actions and options. Though they're still dealing with numbers, they're able to provide forward-looking "what if" scenarios.

Psychologist (an auxiliary member)—a concession to the reality of family businesses. Good psychologists or psychiatrists are ancillary members of the council, even though they are usually in the best position to understand family-system dynamics. They are ancillary members because they *should not* be needed. If they are, they should be brought in only as long as needed. The presence of psychologists on the Council of Advisors is a concession to the usual dysfunctionality of family businesses.

Unfortunately, a psychologist's intervention is only a bandage, not a cure. If the pathology goes too deep, it cannot be fixed so long as the family business exists. A good therapist might be able to help a family if it were not also working together, but its entanglement in the business adds too many problems to the situation. In such a situation, condoning their continuing to work together is like giving heroin to addicts who have checked themselves into a detox program.

YOU NEED THE THERAPIST'S EXPERTISE, NOT THERAPY

Since a critical tenet of this book is that family baggage is usually what kills family businesses, it may seem strange that psychologists are listed as only ancillary members of the Council of Advisors. That's because there's always the danger that the psychologist will want to play therapist. The knowledge of psychology is needed, but not the application of therapy.

Maybe you should throw the baby out with the bathwater. When it comes to business, the best thing to do is to cut all of the baggage out of the business, not try to heal it. This means selling the business—cutting the family out of it—if the baggage is so severe that it's jeopardizing the health of the business.

The business should not have to accommodate the family baggage, although many families insist upon forcing this option on their business (and their family as well). It is a last resort because you can't heal yourself as a family and simultaneously run the family business. It just doesn't work that way.

Have your advisors read this book? If the members of your Council of Advisors have read and understand this book, they'll have sufficient expertise to recognize, diagnose, and address the family baggage that is killing your family's business. For that reason, you shouldn't need a psychologist as a full member on your council.

THE ROLE AND BENEFITS OF A COUNCIL OF ADVISORS

A properly functioning Council of Advisors provides important benefits to family businesses.

Provides the sophisticated business expertise you need. Family businesses continually claim that they lack the sophisticated business expertise needed to be effective. By creating a Council of Advisors, they can gain possession of the expertise they need. They will then be on a competitive par with larger and more sophisticated businesses.

Family members no longer need to ask themselves, "I wonder how other companies do such-and-such?" Their advisors will be able to tell them. Then family-business owners can focus their attention on running the business.

Holds people accountable for business performance. If the family will allow it, the council can help keep the family business honest and force the family to act like businesspeople.

Council members can work with the owners and senior managers to identify goals and objectives for the coming year. In addition, they can perform periodic reviews to monitor the business's progress toward meeting those goals. Finally, they can give performance feedback to the owner and other selected managers regarding their success in meeting their goals, and can also help advise them on performance-related compensation issues (e.g., bonuses).

An objective evaluation of ideas and perspectives. If properly recruited, your council will consist of highly knowledgeable professionals with diverse experience. Because of their backgrounds and knowledge and the fact that they are not enmeshed in the day-to-day details of the business, they can provide objective advice to the business's owners.

Due to many family-business owners' need for control and their tendency to hold information back, council members may be the only people who have sufficient information, coupled with business expertise, to judge the owners' actions. As outsiders, they may also be the only people who feel safe to give the owner critical feedback when appropriate.

They enforce people's roles. As dispassionate observers with business expertise, council members can quickly recognize when people are not adhering to their formal business roles (and best business practices). They can and should bring this to the immediate attention of all persons concerned.

Applies pressure to perform evolutionary succession. The obstacles—both real and imaginary—to performing succession properly are enough to keep most family businesses from doing so. Since few owners or their children are sufficiently motivated to prepare for succession, often outsiders are the only people who can and will put enough pressure on the owner and others to keep this process moving.

They're a resource available to the business in case of revolutionary succession. No matter how well a company has planned, revolutionary succession may be thrust upon it. In such a situation, a Council of Advisors represents a resource that is immediately available to step in and provide quick assistance.

Council members already know the family's business and have sufficient knowledge to make good decisions. Their judgment will not be clouded by the emotions that often hamper successors (e.g., grief at a family member's death). Finally, they can facilitate the transition by continuing to work with and advise the successors, helping to bring them up to speed quickly and thus minimizing the slump the business will experience.

If revolutionary succession occurs, any money that has been spent on a Council of Advisors will more than pay for itself.

20

Create a Strong Team to Run the Company

The success of the family business depends upon the strength of the people running it, both the family members and the non-family managers. Skills that contribute to managing a family business effectively are often quite different from what you may expect.

Create Family Members with Three-Dimensional Skills

The most effective family members working in the business are the ones who possess more than just job skills. They're "Three-Dimensional People" because they have a set of skills and traits that correspond to three separate dimensions. Just as every time you add another dimension to an object your ability to view and understand it becomes more complete, people become more complete every time they add another dimension of skills.

The skills of a three-dimensional person are outlined in Figure 9. A person lacking mastery of any dimension will not be an effective manager. For example, someone might understand the company and what it needs to do (the first dimension) yet have a lack of humility (the third dimension) that has a disruptive effect.

All those working in a family business need to examine their own abilities along each of these dimensions.

SKILLS RELATED TO JOB PERFORMANCE—THE FIRST DIMENSION

These are the traditional skills that are taught to people working in family businesses. Where most family businesses fail is that this is the only area they pursue. In fact, many of them

FIGURE 9

The Skills of a Three-Dimensional Person

**First Dimension: Skills Related to Job Performance
(Traditional job skills)**

- Company-specific information
- General business and industry knowledge
- Leadership and management skills

**Second Dimension: Life Skills
(Ability to cope with the situation)**

- Ability to adapt to changes
- Conceptual skills
- Comfort with current stage of life

**Third Dimension: Character Traits
(Motivation with a balanced ego)**

- Self-reliance
- Personal accountability
- Humility

Person becoming more "complete"

make the mistake of concentrating only on the first element in this dimension—company-specific information—and don't even move on to the other two elements. They somehow think that preparing someone for the family business means solely learning about their business.

Company-specific information. People need to know how their family's business works—the nuts and bolts of how things function. This is basic knowledge, but the danger is that it can be far too narrow.

It's important that family members understand how the business operates so they can understand and troubleshoot problems employees bring them. But the key is that family members shouldn't allow themselves to become overwhelmed with all the technical details—that's what employees are for. As the leaders of the company, they need to know enough to understand what questions need to be answered to solve problems.

General business and industry knowledge. A family business is supposed to be *in business*—in theory, anyway. This means that its owners must have an understanding of key business information. For example, it's helpful to know a little accounting, some finance, marketing concepts, strategic planning, and so on.

It's also helpful to learn about the industry, such as the key trends and what major competitors are doing. Again, the object isn't to master every detail but to have a good overview.

A good understanding of one's industry, combined with an overall knowledge of general business principles, gives business owners a benchmark to use to evaluate how well their company is doing. In addition, it helps them understand the big picture and the options available to them. It's generally not a good idea to have someone who knows only very technical details about one aspect of the company's operations trying to run the business.

Leadership and management skills. This is the final aspect of job performance skills that needs to be developed. The first two elements help business owners understand how their business operates and provides them with sufficient business skills to know what should be possible. This final set of skills enables them to help get their company where they want it to go.

Leadership and management skills include being able to set a direction for the company, to give good feedback and coaching that helps develop and improve the skills of others, and to set goals and hold people accountable. These skills often take the longest to develop, so family members should begin working on them as soon as they enter the family business.

LIFE SKILLS—THE SECOND DIMENSION

This dimension of skills is closely related to people's psychological health. They emphasize their ability to cope with any given situation.

Ability to adapt to changes. People often fail to adapt to the changes in their role as they are promoted. This inability to adapt hampers their ability to be successful. Specifically, when family members enter the business they often do very technical, hands-on work. If they someday become successors, they're going to have to learn to delegate the work. In other words, they're going to have to become comfortable—to successfully cope—with not having direct control over situations and with getting things done through other people.

In addition to personally adapting to change, family members have to be comfortable with implementing changes in the business. Their company is often in competition with non-family businesses that won't hesitate to change, but the influence of the family system in the business may inhibit them from making needed changes. Their business's viability is undermined to the extent that their family system biases them against implementing change in the business.

Conceptual skills. Everything seemed straightforward when they entered the business and were learning how to use the photocopier. Now that they're at the top, everything is "fuzzy."

The nature of problems that people face at the top of the business become less clear-cut. Instead of a simple solution, there are often several options and incomplete or conflicting data. Solving these problems requires the use of conceptual and abstract thinking to see all sides of a problem. In addition, managers have to learn to cope with the nature of these new problems. They cannot insist that there's a simple solution to every situation.

Comfort with their current stage of life. However abstract this skill may seem, it's important for all family members to be aware that what goes on in their private lives or their minds impacts their ability to do their jobs and hence the family's business.

For example, if the kids are just entering the business, they're having to learn how to interact with people within that business as well as adjust to the working world. If they're middle-aged and taking over the business, they have a different set of problems. Finally, if they're about to step aside, they face another set of issues altogether.

CHARACTER TRAITS—THE THIRD DIMENSION

This grouping of traits and attributes goes beyond the ability to cope and relates to people's inner drive and motivation, and, more important, to their ability to control their ego.

This dimension is often overlooked, yet it is critical in family businesses. For example, a father who owned a series of car dealerships had a son who can only be described as a spoiled monster. He bought this son his own auto dealership. While the son clearly had the intelligence to succeed, his ego was larger than the car lot. The top salesmen and the service manager left (i.e., were driven out), and the business failed.

Self-reliance. People who are self-reliant know they have the skills and ability to find employment elsewhere. Rather than cower in fear and hope that nothing happens to their family's business, they're able to focus their energies on doing their job. More important, they don't feel trapped. If they find that they're no longer interested in working in the business or the baggage becomes too much, they can always leave.

Personal accountability. Family members need to be held accountable, and it's easier to do this when people don't spend all their energy yelling "It's not my fault!" Family members need to understand that their actions have consequences, and they need to accept responsibility for any mistakes they may make. They also need to hold themselves accountable for good job performance.

Humility. A lack of humility undermines the business because it is harmful to employees' morale. Family members can never assume that they are somehow better than others or walk around with a sense of entitlement. Instead, they must conduct themselves with proper dignity and have a sincere appreciation for the contributions of others, understanding that it is the hard work of others that makes money for the company.

STEPS TO HELP CHILDREN BECOME COMPETENT THREE-DIMENSIONAL MEMBERS OF THE FAMILY BUSINESS

Parents can take certain actions to help promote the development of positive character traits in their children who are slated to become successors.

Maintain a modest lifestyle that avoids overindulgence. Business owners often love to reward themselves for all their hard work. They do this by living a lavish lifestyle and indulging their children's whims.

Families that are able to retain a more modest lifestyle seem to produce children who are better able to assume the responsibilities of working in the family business and eventually become successors. In addition, maintaining a modest lifestyle often provides a family with a greater sense of financial security, which in turn should help provide a more secure home environment.

Provide opportunities for children to make—and learn from—mistakes. However unpleasant it may be, making mistakes provides people with a potentially valuable learning opportunity. The key is not to focus on why the mistake was made, which is tantamount to assigning blame—but rather to understand how it happened and what steps can be taken in the future to prevent a recurrence. People do not learn if they don't occasionally make mistakes.

If people don't make mistakes on the job, they're either

doing work that is far below what they're capable of or they're not pushing themselves to excel. (Note: I'm not talking about sloppy mistakes, I'm talking about situations where they have to take action and exercise judgment.)

Have children perform basic jobs. Family members who work in the family business need to feel that no job is beneath them. Having children perform basic jobs in the business should help them appreciate the work that others do.

Some owners take this concept way too far and have their children performing the most menial tasks under great pressure. This doesn't teach them appreciation of anything; it only makes them resentful.

Pay them market rates for their work. There's a tendency for family-business owners to pay their children one of two extremes: excessively high or excessively low. Whatever happened to prevailing market rates?

Overpaying children gives them an artificial sense that their efforts are worth more than they really are. It may also make them dependent on the family's business because they certainly won't make that kind of money elsewhere. On the other hand, underpaying children breeds resentment and anger, and it should because this is an exploitative situation.

The best rule is to pay children what an outsider would be paid to do the job because they need to understand exactly what their labor is worth. If they want to, parents can give their children a stipend from the business's profits, but the children will need to realize that this money is one of the benefits of having a healthy, profitable business.

Provide children with honest and objective feedback on their performance. People need to know what their shortcomings are before they can begin to work to overcome them. If they don't, they may eventually become successors possessing these same flaws and weaknesses.

A good rule is to have a senior manager in the company perform the role of mentor and give this feedback. But doing so requires a senior manager who is in a very secure position in his or her job—a person who won't be fired or suffer negative consequences just because the child doesn't like what he or she has been told. If there's sufficient baggage in the business, no such person will exist and the family will need to use an outside advisor to perform this function.

The Elements of an Effective Management Team

Unless we're talking about a small mom and pop shop, family businesses need a strong team of nonfamily managers. This group plays a crucial role in making a business successful. The business cannot afford a weak management team.

THE CHARACTERISTICS OF A GOOD MANAGEMENT TEAM

Four characteristics will help provide the business with the strong management team it needs. Owners must look at these criteria and ask themselves two questions: First, what are they doing to ensure that these criteria are met? Second, are they doing anything that might sabotage them or keep them from being achieved?

Managers must possess three-dimensional skills. With the exception of some minor modifications, the same skills and traits needed by family members in the business are needed by the nonfamily members of the management team.

Managers will only be as strong as the skills they possess. While other things (such as the family baggage) may get in the way of their job performance, their performance can never exceed their skill levels.

Performance is absolutely crucial—loyalty to the family is secondary. Ideally, a group of the best-performing managers that can be found should be assembled. If the owners are really smart, they'll find a group of managers who are a lot more capable than they are. Not only will the business be a lot stronger, but they'll even make the owners look better in the process. Whether any of these managers is loyal to the family is irrelevant.

Most family businesses have a very serious problem: they have a group of marginally capable people who are strongly loyal to the family serving as their management team. It doesn't matter how strong these people's loyalty to the family is, their lack of abilities limits their ability to support the owner and the family.

A broad age range. Having a group of managers who span a broad age range tends to promote diverse thinking, which in turn promotes better ideas that help to strengthen the business. In addition, the existence of younger managers means that people are being developed to replace the older ones, who might be nearing retirement. The last thing a business needs is a bunch of stodgy managers who are just counting down the days till they can move to Sun City.

The existence of outside advisors. Although these people are technically not part of the company's management, they are key members of a good management team.

Outside advisors provide a resource for new ideas and information to be injected into the business, as they possess expertise that is not otherwise available. In addition, they can offer an objectivity that is not always available to people who exist within the business system.

HOW NON–FAMILY MEMBERS CAN PROTECT THEMSELVES FROM THE FAMILY'S BAGGAGE

Nonfamily managers (and employees) need to shield themselves from the effects of the owners' family baggage.

Be competent. Non–family members must maintain their competence and actively keep their skills polished. The more competent they and their performance are, the more valuable they are to the family. In addition, competence should help them have a greater sense of security because by maintaining it they will not become obsolescent and unemployable elsewhere; they will be able to keep other options open.

Stay out of family stuff. One of the biggest mistakes non–family members can make is to try to become bellboys who carry the family's baggage. Being a bellboy is ultimately a no-win situation. This means that whatever the non–family member's involvement, even if only trying to serve as a mediator, at least one side—the loser—will blame them when it loses. The winning side may also blame them for "meddling."

If getting involved in family issues is essential to success in the business, it is a clear warning signal that the owners are rewarding loyalty—being a bellboy—over competence. Staying in such a business will stifle nonfamily managers' personal growth and employability elsewhere.

Work to develop the successors. Since a nonfamily manager will never be put in charge of the company, the success of the business will eventually rest on the shoulders of some family member. Non–family members' jobs will exist only so long as the company is viable, and the company's viability is dependent upon the competence and ability of the successors.

Non–family members need to work actively to develop the skills of the person(s) who will eventually become boss. The stronger that person's capabilities, the greater the probability the company will be able to continue to give non–family members jobs.

Use outside advisors to increase non–family members' influence. Family businesses often retain accountants or other advisors. These people should be hired to provide expert advice, not loyalty to the family. They should respect competent managers, and be utilized as sounding boards to help critique ideas. In addition, they are potential advocates of good business ideas presented by non–family members.

Live beneath your means. There's a tendency for family businesses to overpay long-tenured managers and for those people to live a lifestyle that makes them dependent on being overpaid.

By living beneath their means, nonfamily managers can build a financial cushion that will help protect them from devastation if they lose their jobs. This cushion will provide them with a safety net while looking for another job, and if they are used to living beneath their means, they won't be forced to adjust their lifestyle should they have to take a pay cut elsewhere. Living beneath their means gives them options.

MOTIVATING NONFAMILY MANAGERS AND EMPLOYEES

Because the family business depends on its employees' effectiveness to make it profitable, the family needs to ensure that they are well motivated.

Protect them from family matters. The family system, complete with its gossip, conflicts, intrigues, and baggage, has a way of spilling over into the business system. Owners need to do whatever is necessary to keep it out.

Nonfamily employees do not want to be dragged into the family's issues; they probably have more than enough of their own at home.

Establish clearly defined roles with full and proper authority. Employees need to know exactly what it is they are responsible for doing along with the guidelines or parameters within which to do it. In addition, they need the authority to carry out these roles.

People who do not have clearly defined roles tend to be ineffective. They may become insecure, asking a lot of questions or failing to take initiative out of fear of making a mistake. They may unintentionally work at cross-purposes with other people, effectively canceling out one another's work.

Base evaluations strictly upon employees' defined role. Employees need to know that their performance evaluation will be based strictly upon their clearly defined role and not upon their ability to engage in family matters. Employees worth having will feel they are paid to do a job, not to deal with family issues. Evaluating and rewarding them strictly upon their formal job definition reinforces this concept. It's what they want.

Provide adequate compensation and benefits. Family businesses have a bad habit of overpaying long-term employees. But this does not necessarily motivate people.

Underpaying employees demotivates them. On the other hand, paying them lavish salaries will not necessarily motivate them. Good compensation has to be accompanied by other factors, such as good overall working conditions, fair treatment, and the enjoyment people derive from the work itself. High compensation alone won't motivate them.

Be honest regarding succession issues and advancement possibilities. The reality is that family businesses often have limited opportunities for advancement because the top spots are reserved for family successors. This limitation, in and of itself, is not necessarily demotivating to employees so long as the family is honest about it.

Some business owners fear they will demotivate their employees by telling them they won't be able to advance to the top; instead, they make vague promises or suggestions about advancement. Honesty is the best policy; be clear and honest about advancement limitations from the very beginning.

21

....

Develop a Strong Team

The Owner Can't Do It Alone

Some business owners take responsibility for developing the people who are supposed to become successors. Unfortunately, few of them are qualified to do this, and even fewer realize their limitations in this area. Rather than producing people with three-dimensional skills, they often turn out successors who are incapable of assuming ownership and/or management responsibilities.

A number of key factors inhibit owners' abilities to develop their successors.

THE ATTRIBUTES OF A GOOD TEACHER RUN COUNTER TO MOST OWNERS' NATURE

Many family business owners are entrepreneurs, and entrepreneurs invariably possess certain strengths—and limitations.

The attributes of a successful entrepreneur. Successful entrepreneurs have a hands-on orientation and want to do things themselves so they can see quick results. Their control is absolute; they must have full control over everything in order to try to determine the outcome of whatever endeavor they're pursuing. They also find fulfillment through their ability to do tasks themselves.

The attributes of a successful teacher. Teaching requires giving pupils hands-off guidance. You can't do people's tasks for them if they are to learn, which means that they have to have control over the situation. In addition, teaching and development are a time-consuming process requiring years of guidance before pupils are fully developed into competent successors.

Finally, and perhaps most difficult of all, being a successful teacher means that the teacher must derive self-fulfillment from watching the improved performance of others. Is it, then, realistic to expect entrepreneurs to excel at teaching?

IT'S DIFFICULT TO GET HONEST OR ACCURATE INPUT REGARDING SUCCESSORS

The only way owners can develop successors is by understanding their strengths and weaknesses.

It's difficult for employees to be honest. The best source of information regarding the strengths and weaknesses of successors comes from their peers, subordinates, and superiors. But do these people feel safe communicating the information they have about successors-to-be to an owner, especially one who's probably an entrepreneur? Remember, an owner is probably also the successor-to-be's parent.

The only way to get this information is through an independent third party, and anonymity must be guaranteed.

Owners are fumbling in the dark with the information they have. Since it's not safe for employees to be honest, what owners usually hear is what people believe they want to hear. This is not a good foundation upon which to base important business decisions.

Even if they know the skills a successor-to-be needs to learn, most owners are not experts at putting together programs that will provide the needed training. This is something that is better left to an outside advisor.

THERE IS AN ASSUMPTION THAT LEARNING ABOUT THE FAMILY BUSINESS IS THE SAME AS LEADERSHIP DEVELOPMENT

They just don't get it. Entrepreneurs' need for control is so strong that they demand to know all details. This need is so ingrained that they never seem to understand that their successors don't need to master every minute detail of the business. The key is to learn enough to know what the right questions are rather than amassing all the details needed to answer questions oneself.

Owners tend to focus their energy on teaching their successors the nuts and bolts of the business while failing to provide the guidance needed to develop leadership skills. The resulting successors are often technically competent but inept leaders. For example, in one home-building company, the father forced his son to continue to master general contractor's skills and wouldn't let him take business classes. "You need to build a solid foundation to run this business," he insisted. What this father failed to understand was that the business had grown to become a large company, and his son needed to know how to run a business, not how to build a house.

The successors-to-be will have to go elsewhere to get it. Many successors-to-be find they must go outside the business to get the skills they need to be competent and effective. This practice should be encouraged.

There are several places where successors can go to develop themselves into three-dimensional people.

Use College- and University-Based Programs

An excellent resource for family businesses is the growing number of "family-owned business" programs that are being offered by colleges and universities. These are a somewhat recent phenomenon and are increasing in number.

These programs use a number of formats, but a typical one is as follows. A group of family-business owners and other key people meet once a month to receive instruction on a particular topic delivered by a series of visiting lecturers. Participants receive reading materials and other resources to help supplement the lecture. Participants may divide up into discussion groups to help process what they've heard and to brainstorm on how they can apply it to their business.

How can you learn more about these programs? Just contact your local college or university and ask if it has any programs dealing with family-owned businesses. You should make a phone call to each of the following departments, as applicable: the Business School, the Office of Continuing Education, and the University Extension Department. Chances are that the program you're looking for is hidden away somewhere in there.

ADVANTAGES OF ATTENDING THESE PROGRAMS

Attending college- and university-based programs has a number of advantages over attending training seminars offered by other institutions.

It will be an education, not a training session. Universities aim to educate people, rather than simply deliver one-shot training sessions. So what's the distinction? It has to do with the durability of what you learn.

Colleges and universities provide an education that involves learning how to think—the ability to learn and master seemingly disparate ideas and concepts and find a way to integrate them into a greater whole. It's this ability to think that enables people to evolve with the changing future.

University-based programs bring in numerous instructors to demonstrate a wide range of new ideas and concepts. Your job is to take this information and apply it to your business—to integrate these new ideas and concepts in a way that has meaning for it.

Teaching is what they do best. The people who run these programs are usually very knowledgeable in how to create meaningful curriculum, which is the art and science of helping you learn. They know how information should be presented to maximize your learning.

In addition, they usually have a wide range of resources to draw from when creating their program. Every faculty member is a potential guest lecturer, and in addition they often know people in the community whom they can bring in as needed.

Your classmates are a potential resource. Another advantage of attending an ongoing program is that participants can get to know other family-business owners. They will come from a diverse range of business sizes and industries, but they'll be united on one dimension: they run family businesses. You thus have an opportunity to develop a series of relationships that can form a support network extending beyond the time you spend in the program. You will have a new group of people to bounce ideas off of, who will understand one another's problems and who can add the insight of a different industry perspective to solving various business problems.

CAUTIONS ABOUT ATTENDING THESE PROGRAMS

University-based programs are not perfect. You need to be aware of potential problems so that you can take appropriate steps to protect yourself.

Those who can, do; those who can't, teach. Although they're knowledgeable, some professors lack real-world experience and perspective. They went from being undergraduates straight into Ph.D. programs. What's worse is that Ph.D. programs emphasize abstract research, which gives students a very warped perspective. You always have to ask yourself: Have these people been too isolated to really know what's happening?

Academicians have a tendency to make things unbelievably complicated. They present highly abstract models and frameworks that might work in a laboratory but that totally break down in practice. The theory's nice, but it can't be applied to the real world. And you didn't know Rube Goldberg was a business professor?

To protect yourself, you need to evaluate what's being presented against a common sense test: Can this information be simplified in a way that makes good common sense? Is what's being presented in sync with the needs of your business? Or is the program presenting information that's relevant only to *Fortune* 500 companies?

"I'm shocked—shocked to find there's gambling going on here!" The faculty at business schools make money—a lot of

it—by consulting. One of the perks of teaching at a good business school is that their university credentials help them market themselves. Their "winnings" are the ability to sell their consulting services. It's just not talked about.

There's nothing wrong with this phenomenon so long as you understand that it's occurring. It may be a win-win situation. It benefits the participants because they're exposed to some of the best talent and expertise on the subjects, and if they have a desperate need for help they've found a good resource. It also benefits the universities because it enables them to attract the best talent available and present a wide variety of topics.

Engage in Experiential Activities

HOW EXPERIENTIAL LEARNING DIFFERS FROM TRADITIONAL LEARNING

We're all familiar with the traditional method of learning: An instructor presents information while we try as hard as possible not to be bored to death. We might engage in an exercise or two to try to demonstrate that we have learned the new skill, then we proceed to go about our day-do-day activities and do our best to completely forget what we just learned.

Experiential learning involves experiencing what it is one is trying to learn about. A good example of experiential learning is a flight simulator: you can learn how to fly a Boeing 747 without ever stepping aboard one. With a flight simulator, the student experiences what it's like to fly the aircraft even though the experience is occurring in a room somewhere.

A key advantage of experiential learning is that it immerses you in the experience of what you're learning about, thereby enabling you to understand the subtle nuances of what you're doing. Effective skills often rest on these subtleties, and deficiencies can be revealed and corrected only when you are actually engaged in the situation.

When it comes to developing skills successors will need, they will find it helpful to engage in experiential learning. Even though the first time they actually take over the controls is at 35,000 feet and there are four hundred people sitting behind them, they'll know what to do and how to do it because it's a situation they've already experienced.

THE EMPHASIS OF EXPERIENTIAL ACTIVITIES

What types of skills can be developed through experiential activities? The answer is any skills that are not concrete—that have strong behavioral elements or involve learning new ways of thinking.

Facilitation. Successors need to learn the give-and-take of group processes within a business context. What are these different processes, and which are the best ones to use in certain situations? They need to learn how to help keep meetings focused while ensuring that people who have information are allowed to participate and contribute.

Diagnosis. Business owners do not always get to solve clear-cut problems. Instead, they usually find confusing scenarios where it seems impossible to determine what caused the situation. But if they can determine the root cause, the solution often presents itself.

Diagnosis is the ability to determine the root cause of a problem. This can be accomplished only when people can distinguish relevant from irrelevant information as they inquire into a situation. This ability is more art than science, and it can be learned only through practice.

Coaching. Giving honest feedback that is both positive and critical is difficult, especially when it takes place in the family business. The best way to coach someone depends on that person, and everyone is unique. It's a difficult skill that requires experience.

There are numerous ways to say something. Can you find a way to give feedback that is the most accurate and also put in a way that enables the other person to hear it? Many people are uncomfortable with giving feedback, which causes them to struggle as they do so. They need to gain sufficient experience to enable them to become comfortable with it.

Initiating or implementing change. Throughout a person's tenure as owner, a family business will need to undergo many changes. The only changes that tend to happen automatically are those that are forced onto the business, and those types of changes are seldom good.

Owners must know when and how to initiate change—how to do so in a way that enables people to support rather than resist it. There are processes and skills that are critical to success in this area, and these must be learned. Owners must be comfortable with both the changes they seek to initiate and the processes they must use to help implement them.

SOURCES OF EXPERIENTIAL OPPORTUNITIES

Experiential learning may occur either within a family business or through involvement in organizations and activities outside the business.

Within the business. The most common opportunities for this learning come from involvement on teams or special project assignments. Team or task force assignments are particularly good for facilitation, providing coaching to others and helping to implement change, while involvement in special projects is a good way to improve diagnostic skills.

Outside the business. There are numerous venues available outside of the family's business. Some of the more obvious—educational programs and professional groups—will be covered in greater detail shortly.

Another option is involvement in nonprofit organizations. They are continually looking for volunteers and provide a good forum for mastering these skills.

Utilize Professional and Trade Organizations

Professional and trade organizations are resources available to your business that can provide opportunities for information, learning, and growth.

Family businesses need to explore these differing groups and involve themselves as appropriate. No single organization is a panacea (despite what it tells you), but involvement with such groups provides an additional dimension in helping make your business successful.

WHAT DO PROFESSIONAL ORGANIZATIONS DO?

A number of organizations have been created to try to help businesses be more successful. Rather than calling themselves "XYZ Company," they tend to take names that sound more academic or achievement-oriented in nature.

These organizations often follow a format that is quite similar to that of university-based programs. People come together for a monthly meeting, where there is a "resource presenter" who provides the group with information. This session may last anywhere from an hour to a day, depending upon the group. After the presentation, there are small-group sessions or a group discussion to help participants find ways to apply the information to their businesses.

A second major goal of these organizations is to have the members act as resources for one another. For example, members take turns giving presentations of their business plans. The group then acts as an unofficial board of directors to critique members' plans and provide them with feedback. In addition, follow-up sessions are scheduled in which the group monitors how well they've implemented the plan they presented. This helps keep people focused on what they said they'd do, overcoming one of the major weaknesses of family-business owners.

Some of these organizations also arrange for one-on-one sessions between the group's leader/facilitator and individual members. This is used as a private opportunity for members to discuss personal concerns that are too sensitive for the group at large.

Two of the best-known of these professional organizations are TEC (The Executive Committee) and YPO (Young Presidents' Organization). Both of these are worth consideration.

ADVANTAGES OF BEING ASSOCIATED WITH PROFESSIONAL ORGANIZATIONS

It reminds you that you are a business. The focus of these organizations is promoting the health of companies. Thus they focus your attention on the fact that you *are* a business and that you need to make money and be successful. Rather than letting you drift on your own, they provide you with a structured format of delivering information to you and engage you in activities that help to reinforce planning and implementation that will strengthen your business.

You're not stuck on a single subject. These organizations tend to offer a wide range of topics in their meetings. This helps people overcome their technical bias, which makes them want to focus exclusively on certain issues or areas within their business.

The continual exposure to a wide range of topics helps business owners address all their problems, not just the ones they want to. In addition, allowing members to critique one another's business plans helps expose each owner to the viewpoints of people with differing perspectives.

Group therapy for business owners who desperately need it but would never do it. Participants in these programs often find that many of the problems discussed during their meetings have nothing to do with business. For the first time, they discover that every other person in the room faces similar problems and has similar baggage. They find themselves in a unique venue where every other person understands some of the problems they face.

POTENTIAL DRAWBACKS OF BEING ASSOCIATED WITH PROFESSIONAL ORGANIZATIONS

These groups aren't perfect. Though the following are not reasons for you not to involve yourself with them, being aware of them will help you mitigate any negative effects.

They don't understand this book. Remember, these professional organizations are focused on helping all types of businesses. While family businesses will be represented, it's unlikely that many people in the group will understand the theme of this book—the evils of family baggage. Thus, they will not directly address the root cause of your problems.

The solutions people recommend for your family's business may be excellent business ideas, but they will often flounder in their implementation because they fail to account for your baggage.

They may be used as a substitute rather than as a supplement. Participation in these organizations is not a substitute for direct consulting intervention in your family business. It is only one element among many in the process of making a business effective.

These organizations do not have the ability to probe deeply into both the family system and the business system, and to understand the interplay of the two. Instead, they take a general approach to overall business problems.

They may be perceived as expensive and time-consuming. Family businesses continually claim that they don't have the money or the time to involve themselves in these types of organizations. They view participation in these types of activities as distractions that get in the way of doing their jobs. I disagree vehemently—this *is* precisely what owners should be spending their time doing. Subordinates should be doing all the day-to-day tasks that owners claim require their attention.

Family businesses need to take a sobering look at themselves and ask how much money they are losing by making mistakes that could be avoided if they were to participate in groups like this. They never seem to understand the full costs of their errors.

They have a profit motive. Despite what they call themselves or how they're structured, professional organizations are really quasi training companies. They're doing what they do to make money, and if family-owned businesses don't join they'll go out of business.

Some of these organizations operate as quasi franchises. Group leaders are required to lead a certain number of groups and a certain number of participants is expected to be enrolled in each one.

WHAT DO TRADE ORGANIZATIONS DO?

Trade organizations differ from professional organizations in they are usually organized around a particular industry or profession. Whereas professional organizations try to help any businesses that belong to them, the emphasis of trade organizations is on promoting commerce in their particular industry as a collective whole or on improving the image of a particular profession.

ADVANTAGES OF BEING ASSOCIATED WITH TRADE ORGANIZATIONS

They keep you in touch with the marketplace. Participation in these organizations can provide your business with an excellent source of information on what's happening in your industry. It can keep you in touch with the latest trends, what your competitors are doing, information about what your customers want, and the latest developments in new technologies or processes. All of this is information that you can utilize when doing strategic planning.

They can help improve your job skills. Some trade organizations focus on helping people to develop job skills related to certain professions. There's practically one for every job or profession.

Many of these organizations offer courses that are more technically focused and job-specific than what's available at traditional universities. Some of them offer certification programs where members can take a series of classes and become a "certified" or a "professional" such-and-such. While these courses are beneficial, they are not experiential education and should not be used as a substitute for it.

While these organizations refer to themselves as "professional," this is a misnomer. They are better classified as trade organizations because they focus on mastering specific technical job skills.

POTENTIAL DRAWBACKS OF BEING ASSOCIATED WITH TRADE ORGANIZATIONS

They tend to have tunnel vision. The focus of these organizations may be too technical or industry-specific. These organizations do not talk about family baggage, and hence do not address family businesses' most pressing problems.

They have the wrong agenda. The primary agenda of these organizations is promoting the industry or profession, not strengthening individual businesses. Their supposition is that individual businesses will be helped as the industry or profession as a whole advances.

Their own interests come first. These groups have a strong interest in conveying how important they are. They want everyone to believe that their organization is critical to the industry or profession and that membership in it is essential. But the people who work for them get their salaries from the organization and need family businesses to believe that the organization is important so that they will join.

22

·············

The Right Consultant Is Critical to Your Success

Family businesses need to bring in outside advisors. The first reason for doing so is that it strengthens the business by providing expertise that is otherwise lacking. Second, these advisors bring an objectivity that helps identify and eliminate problems caused by family baggage.

Solo Practitioners and Boutique Firms Provide Your Best Consultants

The best consultants for most family businesses can be found among small-sized firms (commonly referred to as "boutique" firms) and solo practitioners.

Why is this? Because firms differ in their areas of expertise, but when they are grouped by size they have very similar characteristics. They tend to fall into three groups: the large consulting firms (including the consulting branches of the Big Five accounting firms), boutique firms, and solo practitioners.

By way of analogy, the large consulting firms are large standing armies, boutique firms are panzer divisions, and solo practitioners are special forces. Any student of military history knows that a large standing army can be outmaneuvered by a smaller, well-trained, and highly mobile force. Most family businesses need advisors who can move fast, hit hard, and get results.

Finally, though there are differences, I'm lumping solo practitioners and boutique firms together because many solo practitioners are not as solo as they appear. The best solo practitioners have developed their own network of peers to help leverage their expertise, so their ability to form a team to work on complicated projects is similar to that of a boutique firm.

ADVANTAGES OF USING SOLO PRACTITIONERS AND BOUTIQUE FIRMS

They reflect the values, talent, and integrity of the owner. Because these firms are small, the owner has a very strong influence on how they conduct themselves. Owners who are talented and ethical and set high standards will demand the same from their associates and will create a firm that delivers accordingly. If you can find this type of owner, you've usually found a great firm.

They are better positioned to work with non–Fortune 500 companies. Because these firms are themselves small, they tend to understand the problems of family businesses better. Thus there is a more natural fit between the client and the consultant. You don't have a consultant working for a large bureaucracy trying to deliver a product that was developed for Fortune 500 clients.

Another characteristic of boutiques and solo practitioners is that they tend to implement their recommendations themselves. These consultants get their hands dirty and work closely with clients. Thus, the personal relationship between the consultant and the client tends to be closer.

They are much more creative and dynamic. Consultants working for small firms usually have more freedom to be creative when attacking clients' problems. In fact, this greater creative freedom is one reason why many consultants working for the big firms view themselves as simply paying their dues until they are experienced enough to go work for a boutique firm.

Don't make the mistake of thinking that consultants at small firms have carte blanche when giving advice (only solo practitioners do). Small firms usually have a protocol they must follow, but these were not developed by some distant committee at headquarters and passed down into their organization. They were developed by the owner (possibly in conjunction with the consultants), whom they see regularly.

In addition, the consultants in these smaller firms tend to know one another better, and are better able to collaborate as a team when serving a client.

You get more for your money. Boutique firms and solo practitioners tend to have more modest offices; therefore they do not have the same amount of built-in costs built into their fees.

The fees charged by boutique firms and solo practitioners tend to be lower than those of the big firms. Even when the hourly rates seem identical, they're often quite different. For example, for the same rate you'd pay a big firm for some kid just out of school, you'll get a much more seasoned and talented consultant from a small firm.

POTENTIAL DRAWBACKS OF USING SOLO PRACTITIONERS AND BOUTIQUE FIRMS

They reflect the values, talent, and integrity of the owner. The same quality that's a potential advantage can be a significant disadvantage. Owners may create a firm that reflects their vices.

Some firm owners can only be described as egotistical, unethical, and greedy. They don't care about their clients, about the quality of the work delivered, or even whether the client's problems are ever solved. Their firms are designed to make as much money as possible, and their only concern is to extract as much as they can from their clients. For example, I know of one firm whose owner took pride in charging the highest possible fees and was upset if a prospective client didn't gasp when quoted the hourly rate.

I've also known of firms that have taken on the aura of cults. This goes beyond the rigid pressure to conform that is found in the big firms; there may be elements of zealousness. In one firm I know of, all consultants are required to undergo an EST weekend (talk about a frightening corporate culture).

They may be one-trick ponies. Some boutique firms and solo practitioners provide highly specialized services; they're niche firms. This is good if the family business's problem is a narrowly focused one, but the consultant has to be capable of assuming the leadership role in the Council of Advisors. Hiring a primary consultant from a firm with a narrow focus is just as risky as putting an accountant into the role of primary advisor.

Who is this person? Anyone can call him- or herself a consultant, especially if he or she is a solo practitioner. It is very important to find out as much information about the consultant as possible.

They might be a family business. A lot of the smaller firms are owned by husband-wife teams—which makes them family businesses. This is not automatically a negative, but care should be taken (by now you know why).

Hiring the Right Consultant

WHAT YOU SHOULD LOOK FOR IN A CONSULTANT

Since most family business owners are not used to using consultants, they do not understand the qualities that make people effective consultants. These attributes and traits are often quite different from what they would look for when hiring an employee, so they naturally don't know to look for them in their consultants.

The qualities presented below should be used as a checklist when selecting a consultant. Notice that these are intangible qualities. They are not necessarily easy to discern, but the best consultants possess them.

Excellent diagnostician abilities. Consultants must be able to correctly diagnose the root cause of problems. Everything else they do is irrelevant if they can't do this because a problem will continue to occur over and over until the root cause is addressed.

The ability to integrate information and ideas. Consultants may be presented with an overwhelming amount of information. Much of it is irrelevant, and that which isn't is often contradictory.

A good consultant is able to distinguish the relevant from the irrelevant and then take the next step: recognize relationships. The ability to integrate seemingly unrelated information is essential when diagnosing problems.

The ability to go beyond listening to understanding. We communicate through language, and language can be imprecise. The best consultants are the ones who can not only hear words but also understand the underlying message. Sometimes, understanding the true message also means picking up on what was not said.

Integrity. Consultants must be trustworthy. They will have access to very sensitive information about the family business and the private lives of all who help run it.

Consultants with integrity will place the best interests of the business above everything else. They should be impartial and objective.

An understanding of business as a whole—not just a segment of it. A key advisor should be able to help strengthen the company, solve problems, and strategize to make the company grow and remain viable. This requires a broad knowledge of business.

QUESTIONS TO ASK WHEN HIRING A CONSULTANT

Where did they go to graduate school? A good graduate school education enables a person to think along multiple dimensions. Such thinking is the essence of effective consulting. While a degree from a specific school is not a guarantee of a person's competence, it's a reasonable indication (so long as the degree is relevant to what he or she is consulting on).

What consulting firms have they worked with? Many consultants who work for themselves started out by working at the large firms, and this provided them with good training and experience. A successful tenure at a good firm gives them a track record that suggests that they are competent.

Do they write books or just read them? Too many consultants read a book, get a few ideas, then run around applying these few ideas to every client. The problem is that just because they've read something doesn't mean they truly understand the ideas.

Writing a book, doing research, or creating a framework forces people to think through their subject matter. They're forced to take differing concepts and understand each one, then put them together into a meaningful whole.

Are they really consultants or just people who are between jobs? A lot of people call themselves consultants but are actually between jobs because they were downsized. This is an important distinction because consulting requires a specific set of skills that someone who's merely between jobs may not possess.

It's a good idea to determine if they're both new to consulting and on their own—this is generally not a desirable combination.

Are they consultants or trainers? Consultants seek to identify the root cause of a problem, then work with clients to solve it. Trainers deliver training courses. In and of itself, training solves nothing. It is one component of a solution, but it is not the whole cure.

Do they strongly emphasize their affiliation with a professional organization? This is a trick question. There is a proliferation of professional organizations offering certifications for just about any skill or profession imaginable.

The problem with many of these certification programs is that they're worthless. There aren't any requirements other than people join an organization, pay dues, and jump through some hoops. There's no effective screening criteria to ensure competence. Look for additional qualifications.

Do they admit what they __don't__ know? The world is complicated, and not everyone knows everything. If they claim to know everything, either they're bluffing (which you don't want because you have to ask yourself what else they'll try to bluff you on) or they don't see the full picture (which is absolutely what you don't want).

Consultants should have the integrity to say "I don't know" because that way they can continue on to the next step and carefully think it through, then find an answer with value. Unfortunately, this is often misperceived as weakness or incompetence by family-business owners, especially if they're entrepreneurs with domineering personalities.

Who did the talking in your first meeting? Good consultants should do most of the listening during the first meeting because they need to gather a lot of information. This doesn't mean they should just sit there. In fact, they should be in control even though others do most of the talking. Good consultants know what needs to be done and will set boundaries to keep the process moving. The secret is for them to be in control without being controlling.

Were they convinced they could help you before they even talked with you? Only after they've listened and asked questions can they know whether problems fall into their area of expertise.

The Biggest Blunders You Can Make When Using a Consultant

Blunder 1: Insisting That Consultants Have Experience in the Industry the Family's Business Is In

Very few things are industry-specific, and the root cause of problems will almost never be something unique to a particular industry. Someone who's been focused on the industry too long becomes desensitized to just how bizarre and inappropriate certain industry-specific actions are. What you need is a consultant with strong assessment skills who can get in and discover the problems—someone with the insight of a child who sees the strange things adults do and asks, "Why?"

You need a consultant who understands business and is able to identify the extent that family baggage is undermining the family business. The baggage is amazingly similar across all industries.

Blunder 2: Insisting on Telling the Consultant Exactly What the Problem Is

Clients who are adamant about what their problem is and who start to dictate what steps they want to take to solve it are going to be trouble. It's okay—and encouraged—for clients to have ideas about what's causing their problems and for them to convey these ideas. But when they're adamant, it's an indication that they're closed-minded and/or controlling—traits that get in the way of finding a solution.

Clients are continually amazed when presented with the root cause of their problems. It is almost never what they expected, which is why the solution has successfully eluded them. Any actions they've taken were to treat the symptoms, but the problem remains until the root cause is addressed.

Blunder 3: Expecting a Magic Bullet

Many owners are looking for a quick fix that will make all of the problems disappear. They don't see that it took many years to create the problems in the first place.

The crucial thing to understand is that true growth and meaningful improvements come slowly. They evolve over time in incremental shifts because they're being built upon a solid foundation. It takes time to identify and eradicate the root cause of problems.

Blunder 4: Believing That Someone with Industry Experience Knows How to Consult

Consulting is a skill. Hiring people who have lots of industry experience but who don't understand consulting is like hiring people who know a lot about anatomy but nothing about surgery: they may know the names of things inside your body, but if they cut you open and try to operate, they will kill you.

Blunder 5: Not Listening When Consultants Deliver Their Findings and Recommendations

Many owners, especially entrepreneurs, are used to being in control. *They* do the talking and give the orders; people are supposed to listen to them. So it follows that owners may find it somewhat difficult to listen to consultants.

One of the most important things owners can do is to listen to consultants when they present their findings and recommendations. This is often very difficult because the information can be painful. But consultants are not there to judge. Their focus is on identifying the root cause of the problem, not making value judgments. It's absolutely critical that owners listen as hard as they possibly can—perhaps harder than they've ever listened before.

Blunder 6: Jumping on a Consultant's Slightest Error or Inaccuracy

No one is perfect, including consultants. Inevitably and eventually, a consultant will make an error. The important thing to note is the relevance of the error. A consultant may make a statement that's slightly off base or there may be a typo in a report, but the overall theme, the situation being described, and the conclusions drawn are still 100 percent valid.

Clients who are looking for innocuous, irrelevant, and inevitable errors do so as a pretext for invalidating things they don't want to hear. They say, "If you were a little off on this minor detail, how can I trust you with the major findings?" This is a classic symptom of owners not being committed to making improvements.

Blunder 7: Not Comprehending the Full Cost of the Company's Problems or Inefficiencies

Few owners understand the full cost of their problems because they fail to account for the full impact: time lost by *everyone* in the company who is affected by the problem, lost-opportunity costs, lost customer satisfaction. Failing to understand how expensive these problems are hurts owners in several ways. First, their business is losing money, but they are not motivated to make improvements since they underestimate the extent of the damage. Second, they mistakenly view consulting services as too expensive because they don't understand the full value of the benefits received when the problem is solved.

Blunder 8: Using the Latest Fad to "Fix" the Company

There's a danger following fads: they never address the root causes of problems. Some improvements may occur, but things will again start to drift because no one ever got to the heart of the problem. Many businesses end up in a cycle of using subsequent fads to try to solve the problems that were not corrected by earlier ones.

Successful businesses are the ones that shun fads and master the fundamentals.

Blunder 9: Being Shocked by the Cost of Professional Services (and Going for the Lowest-Cost Provider)

Professional services entail professional fees. Many family businesses are not used to using professional services. The sticker shock may overwhelm them and prevent them from using outside advisors.

Even if they don't have the rich trappings of the big firms, the best consultants still incur hidden costs. Since most are self-employed, they must fund their own retirement accounts, pay their own insurance (professional and medical), fund their own pensions, and so on. They also need to invest in continuing education and development activities.

Good consulting comes at a price. It takes years to develop and is something family businesses usually lack.

Blunder 10: Using a Consultant to Placate People

It's dangerous for owners to use consultants to placate employees, family members, or other people associated with the business by pretending to want to address problems. Doing so creates false expectations that will generate resentment when they're not met.

Unless owners believe that a problem exists or have a sincere desire to find out *and then work hard to fix it*—they shouldn't hire a consultant. They'll be worse off than if they had done nothing because they'll have wasted money and disappointed other people.

23

....

Additional Sources of Expertise

Family businesses should choose their prospective advisors carefully to be sure they have the resources and expertise needed to address the business's challenges.

Accountants

Even though most family businesses do not use outside advisors, when they do decide to get help, they overwhelmingly use accountants. These accountants tend to be either solo practitioners or members of a small practice.

ADVANTAGES OF USING ACCOUNTANTS

Though their primary function is to advise you in a narrow field of expertise, a good accountant will be a valuable member of your team of advisors.

They are focused on the bottom line. Accountants are focused—more likely fixated or obsessed—on a company's financial bottom line. Since family businesses tend to do everything possible to keep from operating like businesses, the presence of accountants as advisors can help inject a little sanity into an otherwise insane situation.

Accountants will determine the financial health and status of the business, and they will alert you to the negative financial consequences of your follies.

They help minimize what has to be paid to Uncle Sam (who isn't a family member anyway). There are actions that can be taken and ways of doing things that will produce tax savings that far exceed any fees paid to accountants.

However, care should be taken not to allow tax-saving actions to drive business decisions. Such decisions should be based on supporting the business's strategy, with steps then taken to mitigate their tax consequences.

They allow owners to focus their attention on what they do best. Family-business owners need to focus their attention on just about everything but accounting issues. They need to focus on such things as growing the business, running and managing the day-to-day operations, ensuring that customers are satisfied, and strategizing for and planning future activities.

POTENTIAL DRAWBACKS OF USING ACCOUNTANTS

Expecting blinding insight from someone who's a CPA. Expecting accountants to understand the human dynamics of a family's baggage is akin to asking for advice on dating from people at a Star Trek convention. Just look at what they've chosen to spend their life doing: looking at numbers.

Business is not about numbers. The essence of business is meeting the needs of customers—people—in the marketplace. You do this by building an organization—people—into a team that produces things to meet those needs. Business is about strategy, marketing, organizing, and so on. If you take your direction from accounting, you miss the whole point.

Their profession requires them not to see the big picture. The profession of accounting is driven by the need to apply Generally Accepted Accounting Principles (GAAPs) to financial reporting systems. Thus, CPAs are fearful of mentioning or doing anything that might possibly deviate from a GAAP. Doing so opens them up to possible malpractice and liability.

Relying solely upon accountants for business advice is okay if your problem fits precisely into one of the GAAP criteria. You're out of luck when it doesn't.

Lawyers

ADVANTAGES OF USING LAWYERS

Most people don't realize that one reason we have a legal system is to help facilitate commerce. One of the biggest obstacles to modernization in Third World countries and the former Soviet Union has been their lack of properly developed legal systems. A business needs a person on its team of advisors who can help reap the benefits of our well-developed legal system.

You can benefit from the pain and suffering of others. Good business lawyers see a lot, especially problems or mistakes that past clients have experienced. A business lawyer can bring the knowledge gained from others' mistakes to your company.

They provide protection in a litigious society. Good lawyers can advise you of your legal rights in any given situation. They're able to create and enforce contracts that protect all parties' interests. When someone doesn't pay, they can collect on money that's legally owing to you. You can also use them to keep others from harassing you.

"What do you want it to be?" Three people were asked the following question: "How much is two and two?" An accountant said, "Two and two is four." A physicist said, "It's hard to tell. I think it's four, but it's all relative." A lawyer looked around to make sure no one else could hear and asked, "How much do you want it to be?"

Good lawyers can create legal entities that help accomplish your objectives, especially vis-à-vis succession issues and estate planning. They are also useful in situations where you want to limit your personal liability by incorporating. They can make things be the way you want them to be.

POTENTIAL DRAWBACKS OF USING LAWYERS

Too many people graduate from law school, which means that there are a lot of incompetent people practicing law. You need to take some steps to protect yourself from them.

Avoid those who are jack-of-all-trades and masters of none. A lot of lawyers will try to handle just about any problem that comes through their door. You need a lawyer who has expertise in business matters. In fact, you may need a combination of two lawyers: a transactional attorney who understands estate planning, contracts, and secured transactions and a good litigator who will fight your battles.

Neville Chamberlain revisited. Like accountants, some lawyers fail to understand the power of human dynamics in family businesses. They mistakenly think that a piece of paper can solve any problem. They create all kinds of detailed contracts and agreements (that only they can understand), thinking that once family members sign these, they'll behave.

Too many people have no business practicing law. I always advise clients to find out where, how, and why their lawyer went to law school. I know it sounds elitist, but you want someone who went to a good law school, preferably full-time.

You also want a lawyer who *understands business*. The best thing to do is to come right out and ask that person whether he or she has a business degree. I went to law school with people who were English and philosophy majors; they are absolutely brilliant and do excellent appellate and legal research, but they do not understand business. In the final analysis, you need a lawyer who can use the legal system to apply business considerations to your problems.

Large Law and Accounting Firms

The traditional client base of large law and accounting firms is big corporations, but only so much revenue can be generated from large corporations. To continue to grow, these firms needed to find new sources of revenue, and they seem to have discovered at least one: family businesses.

ADVANTAGES OF USING LARGE LAW AND ACCOUNTING FIRMS

The problems facing your family's business may be better addressed by these large firms, for several reasons.

They're everywhere you are. This is an advantage that's limited primarily to family businesses that are themselves very large or geographically dispersed.

A large law or accounting firm is best able to quickly and cost-effectively respond to your problems wherever you do business because it has a large network of offices nationwide (and often worldwide). Their close proximity to wherever you are helps avoid the costs of traveling to remote locations. In addition, they probably know the local rules, regulations, and procedures and may also have a sense for the local community.

They represent a collection of people with specialized expertise. These firms often have groups of people with high levels of specialized expertise working for them. If your business is facing a complicated problem, they can bring this expertise to bear. As a general rule, they are good to use if your family has a complicated business or if it is involved in international operations.

They are a magnet for graduating yuppies. Large law and accounting firms attract some of the best talent from the best schools. These "kids" are sharp, energetic, and eager to attack clients' problems.

POTENTIAL DRAWBACKS OF USING LARGE LAW AND ACCOUNTING FIRMS

They tend to gaze into the wrong crystal ball. By their nature, large law and accounting firms are structured to service the large *Fortune* 500 companies. This is their orientation, and they will bring certain biases with them when they work for you.

Much like accountants with their GAAPs, such firms will

tend to apply solutions to your company that best match the needs of very large companies, and you had better hope that your problems match their templates. But if your company is a small, rapidly growing family business, does it have the same problems as a Fortune 500 company that needs to be reengineered?

They may be hired for the wrong reasons. A motivation for CEOs of large corporations to use large law or accounting (or consulting) firms is that they are the safe choice. In addition, the impact of expensive professional services is not that significant to a very large company's profits. But how many family businesses are in a position where high professional fees won't have a significant impact on the bottom line?

Guess who's paying for all their expensive trappings. Large firms have posh offices in prime real estate. In addition, their top partners tend to belong to exclusive private clubs, entertain clients with tickets to expensive sporting events, and so on. They do this because they feel their clients insist that they project a certain image. The result is that they have a high overhead cost structure built into their rates.

Large Consulting Firms

These are treated as a separate resource because they offer a broader type of service—insight and advice (in theory, at least)—whereas law and accounting firms tend to be more specialized.

ADVANTAGES OF USING LARGE CONSULTING FIRMS

All the advantages of using the large law and accounting firms (if your family's business is large, complicated, and geographically dispersed). The key is the size and complexity of your family's business. Large consulting firms have a network of offices, they have people with specialized expertise, and they attract good people graduating from some of the best schools.

They can provide long-range industry studies and forecasts. Large firms often undertake large studies on behalf of large corporations to try to identify key trends. The sheer size of the undertaking gives them an advantage. In addition, they often sell the results of these large industry studies to others, and the information in these reports is expertise that can be tapped.

While I have concerns about their ability to look into your company and identify the root cause of your problem, long-range studies and forecasts can be a good resource as part of sophisticated strategic planning.

POTENTIAL DRAWBACKS OF USING LARGE CONSULTING FIRMS

All the vices of the large law and accounting firms. These firms have high overhead rates reflected in their fees, a treadmill that forces their associates to bill, the tendency to throw a lot of bodies at problems, and kids just out of school who are learning at your expense. You will pay top dollar for whatever they give you.

They also tend to use services and methodologies based on their work with very large companies. Their people are required to use preset formulas and templates and have no discretion to deviate.

They tend to have double tunnel vision. Most (if not all) of these firms organize themselves along two dimensions. First, they group themselves according to industry. Second, the people within each of these industry groups specialize according to a technical function. I call this double tunnel vision because everyone is so compartmentalized that no one can step back and see the overall picture. This guarantees that they will be chasing after symptoms rather than addressing root causes of problems.

The reason they organize themselves by industry is that it helps them sell their services by taking advantage of large corporations' own organization into industries. But there is seldom any problem that is killing a business that's industry-specific.

They think that buzzwords equal market share and revenues. Large consulting firms deliberately create new buzzwords and management trends because if they're successful they can position themselves as experts and sell lots of services. Properly hyped, a good trend will make the partners rich for a decade, until one of their competitors creates the next buzzword. Do you think it's coincidence that the reengineering trend of the nineties was started by people at a large firm who wrote a book? Guess which firm made a lot of money selling reengineering services?

24

....

Put It in Writing

There are certain written documents that, when properly used, minimize problems by helping to clarify expectations. The lawyer on your Council of Advisors will be able to advise and prepare these for you.

Prenuptial Agreements

Warning: Spouses may be hazardous to your family business's health. The key is first to understand this fact and then to take steps to eliminate the danger. A prenuptial agreement is a critical tool for accomplishing this.

THE TYPE OF PARTNER DETERMINES THE POTENTIAL FOR DANGER ("ARE YOU A GOOD WITCH OR A BAD WITCH?")

Marriage creates a partnership. The type of partnership created has a direct impact on the family business because there is a direct correlation between the new spouse's level of involvement and the potential for that person to damage the family's business. This is illustrated in Figure 10.

FIGURE 10

The Type of Spousal "Partner" Determines
the Potential for Danger

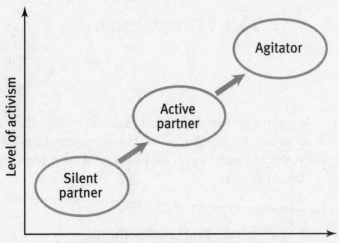

The silent partner: inevitable and healthy. Marriage is supposed to be a partnership, so at a minimum spouses will be "silent" partners in the family business. This type of partnership can actually be healthy for both the business and the marriage.

Silent partners are spouses who do not get involved in the family's business. Either they have their own career in another field or they're playing a domestic role (or both). But they do not work in the family business, they have no desire to, and they don't really want to know what's happening with it. (My advice to people working in family businesses: find these people and marry them.)

The active partner: playing with dynamite. Spouses who are active partners are more directly involved in the family's business. Either they work in the business, or if they don't they actively advise their spouse on what the family should be doing with the business.

A spouse who works in the business brings the possibility of conflicting loyalties, conflict with others, and resentment. A spouse who actively coaches his or her partner is also potentially dangerous, though the danger is not always readily apparent. The coaching may not be in agreement with the party line at the business, and other family members won't like what they hear even if what they hear is the truth.

If the active partner is correct and the family is running the business poorly, the spouse should depart the business and go work someplace else—someplace with a future.

The agitator: to be shown no mercy. Even though to all appearances the agitator's level of active involvement may not be any greater than that of active partners, it is the nature of their involvement that is destructive.

Agitators feel entitled to the family's business, even though they merely married into the family. They want it all, and they will stop at nothing until they get their way. Often they're ill informed, have no understanding of business, and are out of touch with reality. Unless they are kept completely out of the picture, they will destroy everything.

MAKE SURE IT'S FOR LOVE AND NOT FOR MONEY

To put the best interests of the business first and to protect the family, three things need to be included in a prenuptial agreement.

Spouses will not get anything from the business. It needs to be made clear that spouses will not receive any income or benefits from the family business. They may be included on the health insurance plan and receive other normal spousal benefits, but they are not supposed to get automatic expense accounts or club memberships. And they're not supposed to be given a job either.

Spouses have no say in the business. Spouses are expected to be fifty-fifty partners in the marriage, but not in the family business. Remember, the best spouses in regard to the family business are usually silent partners.

Spouses have no claim to the business. This is nonnegotiable because of the harm spouses can inflict. The prenuptial agreement should be structured so that the business is off bounds in case of a divorce or death. The key is to protect the business's viability and to insulate it from disruptive events. If there are other owners, they need to have first rights to purchase ownership, and they should be given considerable flexibility to accomplish this.

Estate Plans and Wills

Laws vary from state to state, so this discussion will focus on the overarching issues.

IT ALL STARTS WITH DETERMINING YOUR OBJECTIVES

The fundamental question in estate planning is this: What do you want to accomplish? Amazingly, many business owners and their advisors fail to ask this question, so their plans fail to address important issues in the family and in the business.

Estate planning is not about money, it's about people. The biggest obstacles to successful estate planning have nothing to do with money. "People" issues create the greatest difficulty. Deciding who gets what, when, and how becomes an emotionally charged process, and it can bring out the worst in the people who are the potential inheritors. It can also cloud the judgment of those who are giving it away.

A common mistake made by business advisors is to avoid the people issues. Moving straight to a financial solution often seems like the easiest course, but the unresolved people issues will inevitably surface and undermine the process.

Ask the kids what they want. Asking the inheritors what they want is important because it helps uncover potential problems in advance. Do they have unrealistic expectations? Are there conflicting desires? If so, it's best to identify and address them sooner rather than later.

Bear in mind that asking the kids what they want doesn't mean they should automatically get it. It's still the owner's prerogative to decide what inheritors get.

The right lawyer can make anything happen. A good business lawyer can use a variety of legal instruments to help accomplish whatever is wanted, be they wills, trusts, living trusts, or other instruments. The key is for the family to determine its objectives; then the lawyer will make them happen.

WHAT IT TAKES TO BE A GOOD ADMINISTRATOR

Many people who serve as the administrator of a family's estate have little prior experience. This is not a problem so long as they possess three key traits.

Integrity. A common ploy of the kids is to claim that the administrator is biased against them. Having an administrator with unquestionable integrity takes this argument away. If nothing else, people tend to give administrators with high integrity the benefit of the doubt, which often defuses many conflicts.

Knowing how to dial a telephone and when to do so. Administrators do not have to be experts on every conceivable aspect of business. What's critical is that they know what they don't know and that they call in people with expertise when needed.

The ability to be a bastard when needed and Mother Teresa when appropriate. A death in the family is an emotional experience, and family members often do things they otherwise wouldn't. Administrators need to be empathetic but are often forced to play the role of enforcer. For this reason, they should be outsiders, not family members.

Outsiders can be more objective and make decisions in accordance with the estate plan. An added benefit is that they don't need to worry about whether they'll be excommunicated from the family system or where they'll be eating Thanksgiving dinner.

MISTAKES PEOPLE MAKE WHEN DOING ESTATE PLANNING

Thinking "I'm too young." People inevitably die—sometimes a lot sooner than they expect. Age is irrelevant. If you have an ownership interest in a family business, you need to do estate planning, if for no other reason than to protect the business (and the other owners).

It's also important to remember that without a will, whatever valuables you have will be distributed according to the laws of your state, and these laws may not distribute things the way you'd want.

Thinking "I don't have any assets." If you have ownership interest in a family business, you have assets. It's not the value of the assets that matters. What's important is that they be distributed smoothly in a way that's beneficial to the business.

Trying to accomplish sentimental objectives. Estate planning needs to be a rational process. Assets need to be distributed, and this needs to be done in a businesslike manner. Estate planning is not the appropriate forum for accomplishing sentimental objectives. It is the time to maximize the total value of what is given to inheritors by putting business considerations ahead of sentimental wishes and by correctly distributing ownership and control to the appropriate people.

Ignoring the Carrie syndrome. If the parents couldn't control their kids while they were alive, what makes them think they can do it from the grave?

Many parents put ridiculous restrictions into their wills. These are preconditions to try to force the kids to behave the way the parents want. Why are these preconditions so ridiculous? First, they violate the basic premise of putting the best interests of the business first. If a restriction does not support best business practices, it shouldn't be mandated. Second, the kids can usually defeat both the stupid restrictions and the entire estate plan in court. Finally, what business is it of the parents what their grown kids do?

These types of restrictions force the kids to go to court to try to invalidate the will. If they are successful, the entire estate plan will be thrown out and there will be a free-for-all among the kids to see who can get what.

TWO REASONS TO DO ESTATE PLANNING RIGHT NOW

They're still afraid of you. Issues surrounding estate planning need to be resolved while the owners are still alive and the kids are too afraid to act up. Even if they don't like what has been decided, they may not be in a position to challenge the owners effectively. However bitter they may be, with the passing of time they may realize that they won't be able to undo the estate plan (because their attorneys have told them so).

This is not what the owners wanted to be successful at. If the owners fail to conduct estate planning properly before they die, all they have done is to successfully create an annuity stream for at least two law firms—the plaintiffs' and the defendants'. And the private investigators. And the expert witnesses. And the court reporters.

Incorporate

Advisors cite numerous reasons for family businesses to incorporate, but there are really only two reasons to do so.

TO SHIELD YOURSELF FROM LIABILITY

The most common reason for incorporating is to shield one's personal property against liability from things the business does. Creating a corporation means that the corporation—not the individual owners—becomes liable for anything done in the course of business. People who sue the business are suing the corporation, not the owners. If they win, the corporation pays, not the owners. The worst that can happen is that the corporation will go bankrupt; the owners will be able to keep their personal assets.

TO LEAVE THE BUSINESS TO THE FAMILY

If an owner wants to keep the business intact and running after he or she dies, it must be incorporated. Incorporating a business creates a legal entity with a life of its own; it continues to live even after its owner dies.

If a business is not incorporated, it literally dies when the owner does because the assets making up the business are the owner's personal property. This personal property will be distributed according to the owner's will or by state law. It's also possible that everything will be tied up in probate. For example, the owner of one unincorporated business was killed in a traffic accident. As she had not yet filed for divorce, state law provided that her estranged husband automatically inherited the business. He sold the company without giving his wife's sisters a chance to buy it, thus putting them out of work.

25

....

Final Thoughts

This final chapter encapsulates the key pieces of advice in this book into a format that can be used on a daily basis. If you do nothing more than follow the guidelines of this chapter, you'll see significant improvements in the functioning of your business.

The Seven Pillars of Wisdom for Family Businesses

Seven principles should guide the actions of all family businesses. Photocopy the list opposite and use it as a checklist to guide your actions continually.

Pillar 1: The Family Is Not the Business—The Business Is Not the Family

A family needs to stop sentimentalizing its business. It's an inanimate object; don't project emotional considerations onto it. Stop the nonsense about how special the business is because your family owns it and how wonderful it will be to pass it on to future generations (because you assume that's what they want). These myths create unnecessary problems. Remember, the business is an asset that will bring value to your family only so long as it is treated like a business.

The Seven Pillars of Wisdom for Family Businesses

- The family is not the business—the business is not the family.
- When in doubt, keep the family out.
- Nothing personal—this is business.
- Maybe the prodigal son was onto something.
- "Unite" and "untie" are completely different words (but they slip past the spell checker function on your word processor).
- Whatever happened to romance?
- It's *not* the economy, stupid (it's more likely the family).

The business is not automatically a reflection of the family. Do not be afraid of acting like businesspeople. If you're the owner, you don't need to be a loving parent to all of your employees. So long as you adhere to good and ethical business practices, you're fulfilling your business obligations. For example, if business conditions dictate that you have to make layoffs, making those layoffs doesn't make you a bad family.

Pillar 2: When in Doubt, Keep the Family Out

When looking for employees, go outside the family. Because of the potential problems associated with employing family members, it's best to err on the side of safety.

This rule forces a family business to operate more like a business and less like a public works program. Owners need to identify the roles needed by the business, define these roles clearly, and then define the qualifications of the perfect candidates. Once they have taken these steps, they need to find and hire appropriate people. If—and only if—a family member best meets these criteria should he or she be hired.

In addition, the family needs to treat business matters as business matters. Not everything that occurs in the business is open to family discussion. People need to adhere to their business roles, and if they don't have a role in the business, then they need to mind their own business and stay out.

To make this rule effective, the owner needs to articulate this philosophy as the company's practice. Doing so will help to prevent problems by keeping family members from developing inappropriate expectations. If family members don't know that they do not automatically have jobs and that everything is not a topic for discussion, why shouldn't they assume otherwise?

Pillar 3: Nothing Personal—This Is Business

Owners need to give themselves permission to operate the family business like a business. When faced with a decision, they should ask themselves this question: "What does good business practice dictate that I do?" They should then do it.

Whenever other family members don't like something, they'll try to impose the family system on the business. They'll make the situation personal: "How can you do such a thing to me? I'm family!" If the owner is applying good business practices to the situation, he or she has absolutely nothing to apologize for.

The object of any business is to survive. The business can't allow the fact that someone happens to be a family member to interfere with what the situation demands—with what would happen if there were no family members involved.

Pillar 4: Maybe the Prodigal Son Was onto Something

As a general rule, kids who want to work for their family's business should not do so until they're at least thirty years old. What should they do in the meantime? Work elsewhere. By being forced to work elsewhere, they will hopefully get the distance they need to discover themselves. In the process, they may learn that working in their family's business is really what they want—or they may learn just the opposite.

A key benefit of this rule is that the kids will get an education in how other companies operate. This helps overcome a typical characteristic of family businesses—that the business will have no new ideas. When the kids do enter the family's business, they'll bring with them a lot of different perspectives, ideas, and approaches. This makes them much more valuable than if they had come straight into the business from school. As a result of this early education in the working world, they'll probably always be aware that there might be other approaches to solving a problem.

Working elsewhere can help your kids learn that they can do it on their own and build their self-confidence. Any successes or promotions come as the result of their own efforts, not because they're the owner's kid. In addition, working elsewhere might help them develop some character and a little humility. Let them be treated as just another employee. Let them learn the joys of working for a mediocre boss. Let them get dumped on just like any other low-level employee might.

Finally, let's look at this from a practical point of view: They'll be somewhat worthless right out of school anyway, so why not let someone else pay them to learn? They need to go elsewhere and make some really dumb mistakes. That's how they learn. Why let them do the damage to your business when there are so many other businesses to mess up?

Pillar 5: "Unite" and "Untie" Are Completely Different Words (but They Slip Past the Spell Checker on Your Word Processor)

According to *The Random House Dictionary,* "Unite" is defined as "to join or combine so as to form a single unit or whole ... to join together for a common purpose" while "untie" is defined as "to loose or unfasten (anything tied) ... to free from restraint."

These words are so close in appearance that you don't need to be dyslexic to confuse them: they both start with the same two letters, they both end with the same letter, and they both contain the exact same five letters. Yet merely transposing the third and forth letters creates two words with completely opposite meanings.

Most family businesses misuse the word "unite" by *forcing* family members to combine into a single unit: the business. People are literally tied up and bound to the business, much like hostages. Research has shown that if you tie up hostages long enough and traumatize them sufficiently, the Stockholm syndrome occurs: the captives begin to identify and ally themselves with their captors. Why should it be any different for family businesses? It just takes longer to happen because this form of captivity isn't as blatant.

Families must learn that the best way to unite family members is to untie them. Remember George Bailey? We met him in the introduction to Part I. He was tied to his family's business, and look what happened. A continual theme throughout this book has been the need for individual family members to pursue their true talents. If these true talents lend themselves to the family's business, they should be employed. But this doesn't always happen, and family members shouldn't try to unite by forcing themselves to work together. Instead, they need to rally around the notion of uniting as a family to help each person achieve his or her ultimate potential.

Pillar 6: Whatever Happened to Romance?

Somewhere in the family there are a husband and wife (or significant other) who are supposed to be lovers. Unfortunately, this part of the relationship is easy to sacrifice to the demands and pressures of running the business. Don't do it.

You must take steps to protect the quality of the relationship. After all, your ability to run the business will be undermined should your relationship suffer. Besides being good for your soul, taking the time to keep the intimate parts of your relationship healthy is good for your business.

Families need to create some type of ceremony that signals that the business day has ended. It needs to be a ritual or a behavior of some type that helps establish and reenforce the boundary between work and family. You need to literally brainwash this into one another's psyches, because unless you do, the boundary between business and work remains blurry and the business day never really ends. For example, I know of a couple who have a practice of lighting a candle. When they come home, they can talk about work until one of them lights the candle on the table. Once the candle is lit, that's it: no more business. Perhaps the fact that it's candlelight helps promote a sense of romance, or maybe it's just that the light from the candle helps to illuminate things a little more clearly.

Finally, creating some type of ceremonial ritual is a way of helping to reinforce the fact that when a family works together, there are two systems present. Knowing that there's family-only time at home can help make it easier to have business-only time at work.

Pillar 7: It's *Not* the Economy, Stupid (It's More Likely the Family)

Family businesses offer numerous explanations for the difficulties they face, but they usually fail to mention the critical one: the family.

This book has clearly demonstrated the numerous ways in which a family's involvement can damage its business. It's time to stop looking outward at things like the economy and to start examining the family's role in your business's problems.

Farewell and Best Wishes

Thus ends our journey together. I trust that you've found a new perspective on family businesses. Hopefully, your eyes have been opened and you now understand what's been keeping your family's business from achieving the wonderful things that people tell you it's supposed to.

I invite you to return to this book and periodically reread it. Not the entire thing, just sections that you feel are relevant. Are you implementing the recommendations? Are things improving? Share it with others in the business. Do they agree?

You deserve the best of both systems (or worlds): a happy family and a successful, prosperous business. This book has given you the way to achieve both.

Go out and make it happen. You deserve it!